LINGERING SPIRITS

CASES FROM THE AFTERLIFE

ANN CARROLL MARTIN

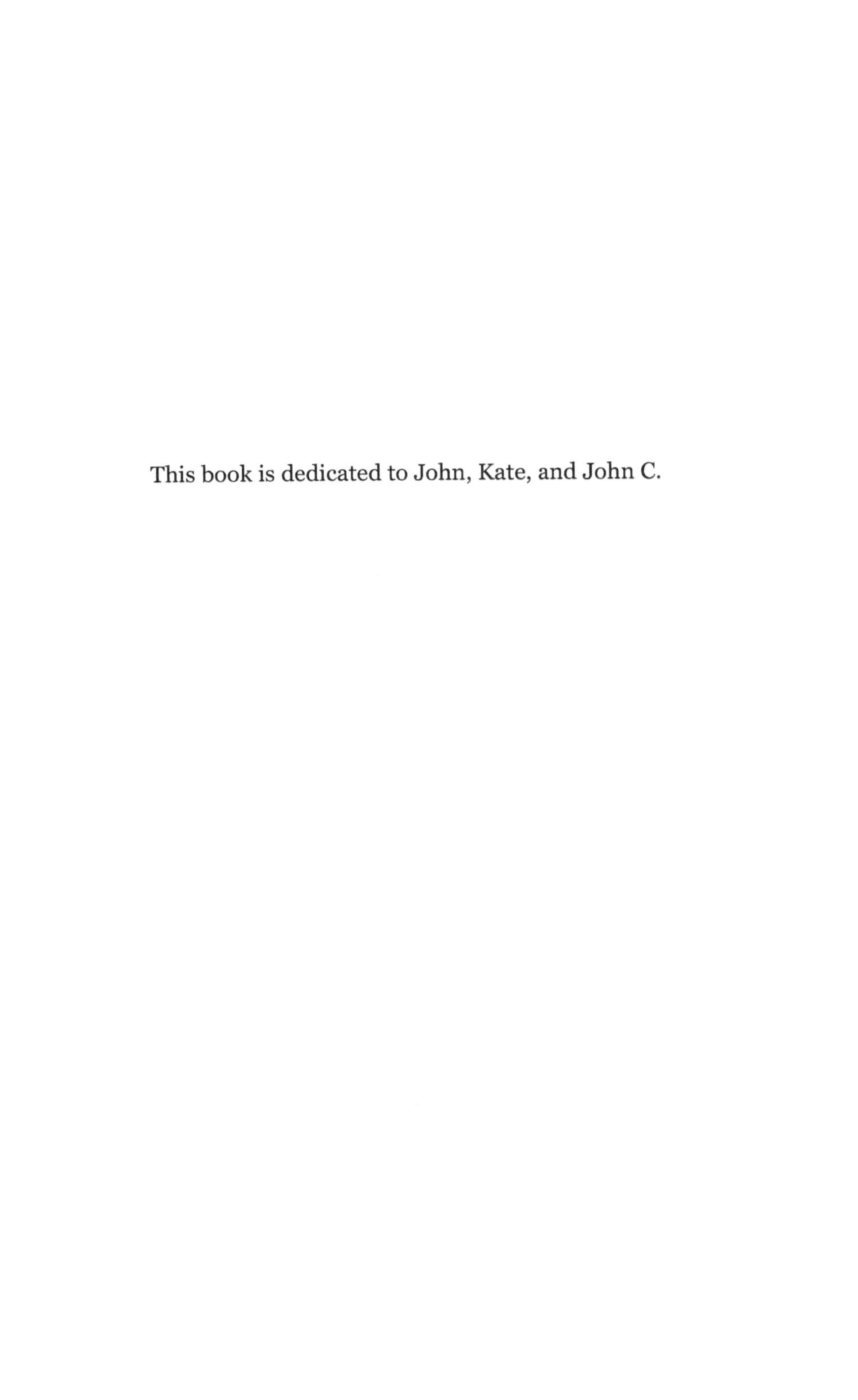

This book is dedicated to John, Kate, and John C.

"For those who believe, no proof is necessary.
For those who don't believe, no proof is possible."
—*Stuart Chase*

ISBN:
Hardcover: 979-8-9883362-2-8
Paperback: 979-8-9883362-1-1
E-book: 979-8-9883362-0-4

CONTENTS

INTRODUCTION

T HERE *ARE* SUCH THINGS AS GHOSTS—contrary to popular opinion and my dutiful parents who insisted upon my psyche that "there are no such 'things' as ghosts." As a child, I had no other choice but to acquiesce to survive inside my high-achieving family into which I had been born. This resulted, at age five, in my banishing all things from the unseen world that I was unabashedly seeing, feeling, and hearing. I begged the benevolent, smiling beings who were my "spirit friends" to go away, and they did, for many years, until the recent past when they returned.

Before I convinced my spirit friends to suppress my contentious gifts, I encountered unfamiliar adults. As I passed by the teachers in the kindergarten hallway, I could unwittingly hear their thoughts: one teacher fretted over arguing with her husband that morning; another complained about how tired she was of teaching; another said she wanted to divorce her husband. I had no clue what any of these adult things meant. They were all talking in their heads, but I could hear them clearly in mine. When I whispered their conversations to my bestie, she balked and proclaimed I was crazy. To feel normal, I learned to block out and ignore that skill of hearing. From then on, I gave the teachers a wide berth in the hallway, avoiding them as best as I could.

Not long afterwards, when I was drifting off to sleep one night, I told the smiling, benevolent faces (my Guides perhaps?) whom I could see in my mind's eye, that they scared me. I asked them to please take away whatever this was in my head, the ability to hear adults' thoughts without them speaking aloud.

For years, it worked, and I could block it out most of the time; I'd hear things but could ignore them. That is until I met my mentor in August 2001. She told me the Masters from the Spiritual Realm wanted me to assist deceased souls. My mentor imparted the technique and showed me how to bring the deceased who are stuck and earthbound to the other side. The modus operandi of the technique is intimate and will remain between her and I.

In the past twenty-plus years, I have heard, seen, felt, and, by using telepathy, communicated and assisted deceased souls or ghosts. Each of the following chapters contains a separate emotional story of how they became stuck after their bodies died. When I find these lost souls, they expose their innermost truth by sharing their deepest desires and heartfelt regrets they experience as spirits.

Who and what are ghosts? Ghosts were people just like you and me, who had lives, but their bodies died. Our mental, spiritual, and emotional consciousness houses the essence and personality of who we truly are, wrapped up together in the soul. After our body dies, our soul survives without interruption in spirit form. Our soul is a "perispirit," which looks like our shape but is gauzy and see-through. At the instant of death, our free will directs our spirit to take action and where to go next. One option is to accompany our spirit guide—a pet, lover, friend, or deceased family member—into the white light toward a higher level, or Heaven. Another option is to remain on the Earth plane. Many spirits go directly into the white light when they see deceased family, friends, or pets they loved and missed and follow them with ease. Those who believe in a Divine higher power are motivated toward a higher level in the afterlife and need no assistance from someone like me.

The spirits or ghosts who do not know where to go because they do not know they are dead are in a kind of limbo. Other spirits stick around people, places, or things. I have encountered a deceased person's soul that appeared through a photograph or portrait. Creepy, right? In their defense, they may desire to communicate with you. That saying "the eyes are the mirror of the soul" is true! One chapter within these pages tells a story about such a portrait.

Heaven, Other Side, Home, Gan Eden, Paradise, Nirvana, Fólk-vangr, Vaikuntha, Mictlān, Arcadia, Aaru, Valhalla, Elysium Fields—all are the one-and-the-same energetic, transcendental place. Many cultures call the next world by a specific name. For the sake of this book, I'll call it Heaven.

What happens to a spirit who decides to remain on the Earth plane? Perhaps they always wanted to visit Japan? Unencumbered by a corporeal body, time, or space, they teleport quickly and easily to Japan! All they need to do is think about being in Japan, and off they go. Another deceased spirit may wish to linger in their favorite neighborhood pub, ball stadium, theater, park, house, boat, apartment, or condo. Perhaps these ghosts wish to be with their loved ones, pets, or business or be nosy and check on their not-so-loved ones or simply be alone. Spirits remain on the Earth plane for as many reasons as there are people on Earth.

The spirits I meet are confused, lost, and/or stuck. Many have experienced an unexpected or traumatic death; one minute, they are swimming in the ocean, and the next, they are lying on the beach, dead from a heart attack. When I meet these spirits, many do not know where they are or that they are dead. As in the movie

The Sixth Sense, the deceased may not understand their predicament and cannot recall the instant of their demise.

For instance, one day, my husband and I were walking along a beautiful beach in the Caribbean. We passed rows of beach restaurants that offered sun beds and rum drinks to the cruise ship passengers to enjoy on the beach.

Suddenly, we witnessed paramedics frantically pumping their hands up and down on a woman's chest, trying to revive her lifeless body. A few minutes later, the paramedic stood and wrote on a clipboard and pronounced the woman's death.

I heard her say to the other paramedic, "Female, in her fifties. Died from a heart attack while swimming in the ocean." She gave the time of death and the date. I looked over and saw a woman in spirit standing ten feet away, looking very confused. Realizing it was the woman's spirit on the bed, I walked closer and began a conversation using telepathy.

To help explain what I do, imagine the third, fourth, and fifth levels of a building. Earth, where we all live our bodily lives, is on the third level. The spirits I encounter are on the fourth level, the Earth plane, but invisible to most. Along with my Guides, we meet and transport the spirits who wish to leave the fourth level and escort them to the entrance of the fifth level or higher level/Heaven. It is up to them to choose to walk across the threshold to their deceased loved ones or pets in Heaven. My mission is to connect with and assist the deceased who are marooned, confused, and lost and reunite them with their loved ones, ancestors, friends, acquaintances, family, or pets already in spirit on the other side.

My mission has been called many things by many cultures. In Greek mythology, Charon, the son of Erebus and Nyx (Night), ferried the souls of the deceased over the Rivers Styx and Acheron. In the Native American Culture, I am known as a "boat woman."

Many shamans and other layfolks do what I do too.

Sometimes I help one or two spirits. Other times I help thousands of souls—for example, after 9/11 in New York City or a five-hundred-year-old indigenous warring culture in Brazil.

* * *

Over twenty years ago, my mentor, Chloe, popped into my life like the wizard Gandalf in *The Hobbit*. Gandalf convinced Bilbo Baggins to leave the safety of his home to go on an adventure. Chloe was my Gandalf, who did that for me. She shifted my life onto "the road less traveled," and it has made all the difference.

Chloe lived in Paris and was visiting a close mutual friend for two weeks where I lived in Connecticut. Chloe is a top executive at a TV station in Paris, the equivalent of ABC news in New York. It is ironic and fateful that her career is in communications. She and I hit it off and began talking about spiritual things. One night, in my home, Chloe informed me the Masters of the Spirit Realm had directed her to transfer to me a spiritual download. This spiritual download would enable me to transport deceased spirits to the threshold of Heaven. She asked if I wanted to do this spiritual work of helping souls. I did not hesitate. I figured when the real Masters of the Universe (not the comic book ones, no offense) ask you to do something, you say yes! I remembered all the spirits I saw but could not help when I was little.

I sat next to Chloe. She told me to close my eyes, and I felt a subtle, gentle energy start at the top of my head and surround me with an effervescence like soda water. She asked if I could feel it. I could, and it felt like a gentle fizz that engulfed me; it was light and wonderful. The process lasted fifteen seconds, but I felt a profound difference and a subtle lightness of being.

The spiritual download has enabled me to communicate tele-pathically with deceased spirits. My mission is to escort these spirits to move from this level to the next. I have never met most of the spirits I have helped to transition, but I have brought over deceased

v

friends and relatives. It has been and continues to be a sacred privilege to help facilitate these lost souls, and I am humbled to serve the souls and Masters of the Spirit Realm. This is my true calling in this life, and I am grateful for it.

I have no idea why the Masters chose me. However, I have always been curious about the world we cannot see with our physical eyes and have been a seeker of this unseen world and read books regarding positive energies: the genre of angels, our soul's journey, the idea of reincarnation, past lives, protecting oneself, and the like. I am curious about invisible energy and the forces around us.

Also, Chloe informed me the spirit world strongly desired that I balance the negative karma I had incurred in a past life. Fortunately, I have no recollection of any of my past lives. But apparently, in one of them, I was a man in ancient times and was in the equivalent of the KGB. I killed many, many folks with a sword! (I fantasize I was that big guy in *Game of Thrones* named Mountain. I am just kidding.) She said the Masters said this karma could be balanced by my helping many, many souls get to Heaven. It sounded like a plan, and I have been trying to balance it since.

As we all know, the start of any new job can be daunting. *What if I fail? What if it doesn't work?* I thought, *How am I going to meet deceased souls and transport them anywhere, let alone to the entrance of Heaven?* I was encouraged by my Spirit Guides to surrender and trust the process. However, I was skeptical. My road from skepticism to acceptance is within these pages. I do not do this alone; several Spiritual Beings assist me, such as St. Michael the Archangel. Some of you may return this book to the shelf and say, "Okay, not for me." I hope you reconsider, as it is my sincerest hope for writing this book that by the end, you will grow less afraid of ghosts, less afraid of dying, and perhaps surprise yourself that your spirit/soul survives after your body dies.

This book is not for the faint of heart but for the courageous-minded to attempt acceptance and the prospect of life continuing after death. These are the stories of spirits, ghosts, or deceased people, whichever you wish to call them. The spirits in this book lingered, became earthbound, and "haunted" the people, places, and things they knew and loved when they were alive. This book contains their stories.

* * *

I was brought up in the Roman Catholic religion. One of the tenets of the flock is to strive to be good and aspire toward eternal life in Heaven. To gain Heaven is conditional upon and adhering to the Ten Commandments, stellar personal behavior, and an abundant supply of good deeds. To commit a sin was to sin against God, church, family, and community. Who goes through life and makes no mistakes? When I was informed that the Masters in the Spirit Realm wanted me, an ordinary layperson, to bring deceased souls to the Gates of Heaven, I pondered this new course of behavior and concluded it was blasphemy according to the Catholic Church. My eternal soul was at stake, and yet the Masters of the Spiritual Realm were asking me to perform this? I was conflicted and struggled with doubt that I had what it took for what the Spirit Guides expected of me.

This created many volatile dilemmas in my little brain. Who the heck was I to think I could bring souls to the Gates of Heaven? How was it possible? I was a woman married to a wonderful man with two terrific children living in a suburb and teaching in a small town. I was not, nor am I, a saint! Just ask my family! I had only read about the Spiritual Realm. There were many "dark nights of the soul," thinking and believing in this new reality. My sanity was at stake. I thought I must be delusional. Was it working when I brought a spirit to the other side? Physically, how could I prove to anyone the spirits were gone? Only when clients told me they were no longer seeing apparitions, hearing angry voices, feeling someone watching them, or moving objects were my misgivings confirmed. The only physical proof I had that the spirits were gone were from my clients feeling at peace in their living space.

I needed assurance and asked for proof from my Spirit Guide. I devised a method to believe I was on the right path. I asked for a particular word or phrase—written or heard—that I would encounter or recognize three times in one day. For instance, I would see the word "bliss," then I would hear the word in a song, then I would see a street named Bliss or the word written on a billboard, or a person in passing would say "bliss." The affirmation had to ring true and sit comfortably inside me. It proved that Spirit was with me when I saw these signs and synchronicities. Fortunately, my Spirit Guide was patient. I felt supported using this method and more secure in accomplishing this work.

Alongside this, I was having difficulty living my physical life and fully incorporating this new spiritual one. At first, my husband was not on board. He thought I had joined a "cult." He tried to be good-natured and teased me but had trouble accepting my "new mission" and jokingly called it "heebie-jeebies." I was having doubts about the existence of spirits, let alone helping them. Finally, I threw down the gauntlet to the Masters in the Spirit World.

I hit my breaking point; my mind stood at a crossroads. Do I wholeheartedly believe in this work of bringing souls to the other side or bag it altogether? I knew for my own mental well-being, I had to commit one way or the other. So I created a visualization. I saw myself standing on the edge of a very high cliff, miles high, like you see in a Road Runner cartoon. In my mind, I stood on the ledge, turned around, closed my eyes, and, with my arms outstretched, fell backward in a free fall into the airy abyss below. I floated gently downward and experienced a profound serenity. I fell freely into surrender, where there was no doubt or fear. It was liberating and felt great. When I opened my eyes, I knew my answer and felt a calm resolve to commit fully to doing this work. I have not looked back since.

I am blessed and confident knowing my Spirit Guide, and I have helped many lingering spirits move forward on their path. It has been the most rewarding thing I have ever done or will ever do in this lifetime, along with living with my husband and children. I am sure there is spiritual life after bodily death. The essence of who we really are lives on in another form, ad infinitum.

I believe we are spiritual beings before coming to "Earth School" to experience and incorporate life. We house a Divine spark within each of us to gain knowledge for the purpose of our soul to heal ourselves and try to heal our relationships before we return to the Divine source. I believe our most difficult relationships are disguised as our greatest teachers. If we reconcile these life lessons here, we will not need to repeat the same lessons in a future lifetime, and our soul will progress.

Each of us is a medium born with gifts to see, hear, and sense the unseen world. It is a subtle muscle that requires intention, attention, and focus. A person who walks into a gym does not get strong by looking at the machines. They need to work their body on the machines to strengthen their muscles. It is this same principle applied when using your intuition. Herein are some of the stories of those spirits whom I have had the humble privilege to facilitate to the doorway of a higher level.

DEFINITIONS

Earthbound: Attached or limited to material existence as distinct from a spiritual or heavenly one. Located on or restricted to land or to the surface of the earth. Unable to leave the surface of the earth.

Empath: A person with the paranormal ability to apprehend the mental or emotional state of another.

Essence: The intrinsic nature of a person that determines their character. The quintessence—the mind, soul, spirit, life, core, heart.

Ghost: An apparition of a dead person believed to appear or become manifest to the living, typically as a nebulous image. I prefer to use "spirit" or "soul" instead of "ghost," which frightens many people. Many books and movies about fearful ghosts have permeated our psyche and culture. The ghosts or spirits I meet were once actual people who are now deceased.

Golden Rule: The principle to treat people as you want to be treated

Guide: Archangel St. Michael, St. John. High-level spiritual entities from the Spiritual Realm who assist me in collaborating with deceased spirits to help them to the Other Side. Other guides are deceased family members—my father and my cousin.

Karma: The sum of a person's actions in this and previous states of existence, viewed as deciding their fate in future existences. Simply put: Good intent and good deeds contribute to good karma and happier rebirths, while bad intent and bad deeds contribute to bad karma and bad rebirths.

Mantra: "I am a being of unconditional love and light. I am at peace and perfectly in line with my destiny." Believe and repeat it over and over.

Masters: The Highest of the High in the Higher Realms; God, Supreme Being, Jesus, Buddha, Mary, Quan Yin, to name a few. A High Realm spiritual entity by any other name.

Mentor: A person or spirit who provides guidance. My mentor Chloe gave me the instructions for facilitating spirits to the Other Side. This information originated with the Masters and was given to her by the Masters.

Other Side: The Spirit Realm or Spiritual World. In this book, I refer to the Other Side or Home as being in a higher dimension. Heaven. Some may argue that the Other Side is not a place. For the sake of this book, the Other Side or our original Home is referred to as the highest destination a soul attains after their bodily life.

Orbs: Round white or clear circles that appear in photographs. In my experience, these are ghosts.

Pierre Teilhard de Chardin said: "We are not human beings having a spiritual experience. We are spiritual beings having a human experience."

Poltergeist: A poltergeist is a ghost or supernatural being supposedly responsible for physical disturbances, such as loud noises and objects thrown around.

Reincarnation: The rebirth of a soul in a new body.

Ring True: Seem to be correct or plausible. Something resonates with you. You understand and can sense it without explanation or problems. Resonance is a common vibration, so it means when two things move in unison, they feel in common.

Spirit: With a capital "S," it refers to the high-level beings in the Spiritual Realm. With a lowercase "s," it stands for the deceased spirits, souls, or ghosts. These spirits chose to not go to the Other Side. They occupy the area surrounding the Earth plane.

Spiritual Intuitive Empath: the ability to sense, hear, feel, and see spirits and know how they feel.

Telepathy: The ability to communicate with someone mentally without using words or other physical signals. Extrasensory perception or ESP.

I

ROMEO AND JULIET

W E BOUGHT A BIGGER HOUSE on four-plus acres as an investment, thinking we'd flip it and make a fortune. We had time before moving in, and my husband made a deal with me: "If you strip off the ugly wallpaper in our future bedroom, then I will pay to have it painted."

Deal.

The bedroom was situated on the first floor, which was bigger than our first apartment. After work, dinner, and our kids in bed, I would drive to the outback of town to work on the walls. To reach the high ceilings, I worked on a tall ladder. One night, I heard children laughing outside in the pitch dark after 9:00 p.m. Curious, I climbed down, opened one of two glass sliding doors, and the giggling stopped. I remember thinking, That was creepy. But I had work to do, and my logical mind did not wish to entertain the notion of unexplained phenomenon in my soon-to-be backyard. From then on, I blared the volume on my clock radio to drown out any outside noises when I worked. Yes, these were the days before iPods.

That next fall, after we were settled in, I remarked to my neighbor how the tall maple tree stood out with its vibrant fall colors in the backyard.

She quipped, "Oh, you mean the hanging tree?"

"The what?" I said.

She recounted the tragic story of a young couple who ran away and made a suicide pact to be with each other for all eternity. The teens' suicide note was found in the pocket of his jeans. They hung themselves on the big maple tree in our backyard a year before we moved there—our neighbors had discovered their decomposed bodies the previous spring. She was only fifteen years old, and the boy was eighteen. The girl's mother wrote a note to our neighbor and relayed the backstory. She had told her daughter she was too young to be in love and that the boy was too old for her. When the mother forbade the relationship, the pair decided to be together forever and chose a secluded spot in our backyard to carry out their love pact.

I did not know back then that the giggling and laughing originated from the deceased teenage couple. It would take ten more years until I could help them to Heavens doorstep.

My mentor, Chloe, explained the importance of protecting myself by asking the highest energies for the highest intention to engulf me. I was instructed to imagine a white beam of light surrounding me and bring the spirits into it. It was also important to ask the deceased relatives, pets, or friends to come and meet the spirits. When earthbound spirits see familiar faces, they willingly go toward them into Heaven.

I could feel the innocent, sweet, loving energies of the young couple. Their demeanor was shy and reticent in front of Chloe and me. We did not have much of a conversation. I sensed it was more about them feeling and knowing our willing energy and desire to help them. It was not about "words" but all about our benevolent intentions toward them.

Chloe and I gently communicated telepathically, asking them if they wanted to go to Heaven. They eagerly agreed to go with us, especially after ten years of being in spirit in my backyard. Together they easily went into the bright light. They saw their passed-on relatives waiting to greet them at the entrance to the Other Side/ Heaven. It was so gratifying to watch the sweet, young couple walk over to their loved ones. They all smiled, turned, then disappeared across the threshold into Heaven.

Wow, I was flying high! I felt energized, elated, and bewildered by this new experience. In the morning light, I wondered, "Could I accomplish this alone?" It was one thing working with my mentor, but it was another to believe I could do this on my own. However, Chloe assured me before she went back home to France that I would be able to accomplish this along with St. Michael the Archangel.

During this time, when I was first learning this new skill, my husband had a "wake-up" call and underwent emergency bypass surgery. He was forty-eight years old, part owner of a business, in a stress-filled job, and smoking three packs a day. The men in his family do not enjoy longevity; their hearts give out younger than most. We decided life was too short, so we reevaluated our lives and gave up our current jobs. That winter, my husband recuperated in Florida. Up until then, I was thankful the Spirit world was quiet. My mentor and I were in touch via email as my hundreds of questions on the method were endless. I was grappling with the thought of accomplishing this new spiritual gift. Shortly after we arrived in Florida came my first chance.

$$2$$

THE LITTLE ANGEL

EARLY ONE JANUARY MORNING, we took our aunt, who was in severe abdominal pain, to the emergency room. It was overcrowded, and we knew we were in for a long wait. As I walked in front of the main desk, the staff began shouting that an eighteen-month-old boy was arriving by ambulance. He had been found face-down, floating in the swimming pool at his home. My heart skipped a beat, and I instinctively thought this may involve me.

I stood in the hallway opposite the ER door. Suddenly, it flew open; the policeman stopped short and looked at me without a word. From the expression on his face, I knew he had found the little boy drowned in the pool. It was a road map of fury at the mother found passed out in a drugged state, sadness at the senseless loss of a toddler, and frustrated anger for not rescuing him in time. I could hear his emotions in my head as clearly as the teachers from my kindergarten days.

The little boy's spirit stood quietly next to the officer. In disbelief, I watched him leave the officer's side, walk over to my side, and reach up for my hand. I could feel his little fingers holding mine; it was clear he wanted to go with me. I was amazed and thought, *Now what do I do?*

I asked my Spirit Guide, "Do I close my eyes and attempt to take him to the Other Side in this busy hospital hallway?"

The answer in my head came back a resounding "Yes!"

The officer left, and I was alone with the little boy's spirit. He did not try to talk to me. I closed my eyes, leaned against the wall, and began the process. Suddenly, the double doors at the end of the hallway burst open, and a throng of people noisily approached. I jerked awake, and the interruption halted the procedure.

Back at home, I emailed Chloe and asked her to confirm if the little boy in spirit was on the Other Side. She said I needed to go back and finish bringing him up. A while later, I took my bicycle and rode to a secluded spot to watch the sunset on the water. It was a gorgeous, clear evening, and the sun sank slowly into the sea with hues of oranges and pinks shimmering on the Gulf. The beauty and tranquility of this moment created a serenity in me that inspired me to finish what I had begun earlier in the day. I closed my eyes and saw the little boy in spirit. Again, I took his little hand in mine. Together, we went to the entrance where I stopped and he walked on ahead. Nothing could have prepared me for what I witnessed as the little boy's spirit grew into a huge winged angel about twenty feet tall. He flew up high and away without a backward glance.

I asked my Spirit Guide for a glimpse inside and was only permitted to take a few steps forward. The colors were resplendent. Everywhere the flowers were brighter than anything on Earth. The grass was a striking green and perfect. The only comparison that came to mind was of a Kodak photo in Technicolor compared to its negative—the Other Side being the photo and Earth being its brown negative film. I opened my eyes to see the last of the sunset and was surprised at how dull it appeared after what I had just seen. Earth is pretty gorgeous, but it's nothing compared to the indescribable beauty I saw in Heaven.

I often wonder what happened to the little boy's mother. I never knew her name nor his. I think of the many scenarios for her and hope for the best outcome. I wish I could have told her what happened to her son when he arrived in Heaven. It is the only time I have been lucky enough to see a small child's soul transform into a very large winged angel. I wonder if all small children transform into angels when they pass? I like to think they do.

3

THE ANGELS CARRIED HIM HOME

O NE MONTH LATER, my eldest brother passed. It was surreal to comprehend my friend was gone for good. His funeral was a hazy nightmare, filled with pain, anger, and grief. Losing a sibling is as if a limb suddenly goes missing, and you wonder where you misplaced it.

I had last seen him two months prior at Christmas, where we typically laughed and joked around the dinner table. It was one of those good times you think will last forever. Whenever someone asked him how he was, he would respond, "Never better." Nothing could be further from the truth.

My brother had been confused and lost since he was a child. I was pissed off to think I could have saved him. I had before, twice. In the end, no one saved him. We are all on our own spiritual journey. Often what's required to maintain a semblance of content-ment eludes us. I knew of his predicament and personal afflictions but never believed he would end his life. No one truly knows another's inner sufferings. Within the dark crevices of the heart exist treasures and torrents that collide, confuse, and take hold. We can make conjectures of the struggles in the heart of another and, in the guessing, be entirely wrong.

On the day he died, my husband and I flew to New York to comfort my mother. We arrived at night, and I spent the night in her house so she would not be alone in her grief of losing her eldest son. I lay in my childhood bed, trying to fall asleep. The same bed where, years earlier, I had asked the benevolent faces to take away my gift. Now I needed those faces more than ever.

Suddenly, my Spirit Guide switched on a vision in my head, showing me what had happened to my brother that morning. I saw him lying on the ground under a tree in a field right after he had shot himself. In the next "frame," two huge winged angels flanked him and lifted his spirit upward as his body lay on the ground. Together all three rose into the air. Each angel held him under his armpit and brought him straight upward until fading out of sight. As he ascended, I could see that my brother's eyes were closed, and his spirit appeared to be asleep. He never woke up as they carried him into the sky and out of sight. I thanked Spirit for giving me this gift, and they responded, "Your brother is going to be alright." I was so relieved and grateful to Spirit that I cried myself to sleep.

The next morning, I started to go into my mother's bedroom to let her know and reassure her that her eldest son was "in good hands" with the angels. I stopped myself because I realized, sadly, she would never believe me or what I had seen. My mother and I got along like oil and water, never quite jiving. She was a good Catholic, but she did not believe in ghosts or angels.

Many know someone who has taken their own life. I believe they all go home to Heaven. Once we walk through the door, the Masters show us our entire life, and we witness our life review, much like in the movie *Defending Your Life*. The life review shows your whole life—your actions and reactions to circumstances. From the time we are born, we are learning and formulating ourselves through our experiences. Each decision we make and situation we encounter allows us to shape who we want to become. In life, the only thing we really have control over is our reactions. How we handle our relationships and how we behave is what our spirit is here to learn in Earth School. During our life review, we can see how we could have done better in some instances and where we did a great job in others.

My brother's spirit returned to me once and told me he could not be here anymore; it was just too hard. We often judge ourselves harshly. We are given impossible standards to live up to but not the tools to accomplish them nor the coping skills to handle the inevitable failure we all experience. Failure is a huge part of learning at Earth School. The proselytizing of extreme morality can send us delicate and loving humans into a shame-filled spiral we cannot pull ourselves out of.

Keeping the golden rule of "doing unto others as we would have done to us" in the forefront of our minds is so important. It's hard in the heat of the moment, but you cannot let your temporary emotions dictate reactions. We are all in this life together, doing the best we can, yet we can always strive to do a better job at loving and being charitable. The success of Earth School is in the striving to be a good person. If we treat ourselves gently, we are more likely to be gentle with others.

4

———

JUDGE NOT
LEST YE BE JUDGED

IN THE EARLY DAYS OF PERFORMING spirit transportation, my convictions were slow to accept I was ferrying invisible entities to another level and that it was all being accomplished via my mind, resulting in no tangible proof. Naturally, I discussed this new venture of bringing ghosts to the other side with my girlfriends, who were my greatest supporters. They had no trouble believing in the idea, and their encouragement spurred me forward!

One close friend, who owned a beauty salon in town, told me a true story involving a high school acquaintance, Jean. Jean and her husband, Mark, grew up in town, met at the local high school, and had been married for twenty years. Both worked at the town hall—Jean in a clerical position and Mark in maintenance. Mark was a very jealous husband and, over time, became physically abusive. Jean was miserable and began to confide in another man at work, Tim. After a while, Tim grew to care for Jean very much and wanted to be with her. Finally, Jean could not endure her husband's abuse any longer and decided to leave him. These were the days before cell phones, but many people used home phone answering machines.

On a fateful afternoon, Tim left a message for Jean on her home answering machine. He explained that he loved her and how happy he was that she was finally planning to leave her husband to be with him. Jean normally arrived home from work first, and Tim believed Jean would erase his message long before her husband got home. Unfortunately, Mark arrived home earlier than usual before Jean and heard Tim's message. When Jean arrived home, Mark shot and killed her, then turned the gun on himself. To make matters worse, their two teenage sons were downstairs, heard the gunshots, and found their parents dead. It was a horribly tragic day for that poor family.

Two years had passed since the incident, and another family of four moved into Mark and Jean's former home. The new couple had two small daughters, aged four and five. Not long after they moved in, the two little girls refused to sleep in their bedroom, claiming there was "a pretty lady with long hair in there." In the middle of the night, their father saw a lady standing by his bed staring down at him. The couple called a priest, and he performed an exorcism in the house. It had no affect as the two little girls still saw the lady in their bedroom, and their father was still being awakened by the lady in spirit.

After my friend finished the story, she turned to me and said, "Perhaps you can help them?"

I responded, "No way." My friend did not know the current homeowners personally, and I was not about to call strangers out of the blue. What would I say to these poor folks? "Hi, you don't know me, but I heard your house is haunted, and I can help." If they were not open to what I did, it would sound crazy. My friend promised to find out their names.

I panicked. It was one thing for me to share my new abilities with my friends, but it was an entirely different thing for members of my community to hear about me as a "ghost buster." I had my occupational status at stake. What if word got around town that I could communicate with ghosts? I thought I would get fired from teaching children, for sure. That being said, helping spirits is my first responsibility. Chloe told me that when I hear a story out of the blue that involves spirits, like this one, then I am supposed to do all I can to help them.

I was used to asking my Spirit Guide for a sign, so I tuned in and asked, "Am I supposed to cold call a couple who does not know me and tell them I can help their house ghost?" I received no reply. I asked again for a positive declaration, and pleaded for a sign, a signal, a word, anything resembling an affirmation. I needed assurance from the Spiritual Realm that calling this couple was the right thing to do. I was perturbed that my Spirit Guide said nothing.

That night, my friend called to give me the lady's name and phone number. Her name was Tessie! My breath caught in my throat, and I nearly dropped the phone. This was my sign—her name was Tessie. No one knew that my deceased father of thirty years called me Tessie. It was his nickname for me. I immediately felt his presence in the room with me. Not only were my Spirit Guides finally giving me the go-ahead sign I had been asking for all day, but my father was letting me know he knew about my spirit work. In my wildest dreams, never did I imagine my conservative Catholic lawyer father would condone this work. Yet here was his approval.

I asked, "Could it be true that he consents to my doing this work?" The answer from my Spirit Guide was a resounding "Yes!" Instantly, my hesitancy was gone.

I was only twenty-two years old when my father died with his head in my hands at home in his bed. My father was my beacon of light to strive toward, my benchmark for morality and ethics, and my best friend. Hearing the coincidental name Tessie reassured me that Pop knew I was doing this spiritual work. This gave me not only the courage to call but also the security in the knowledge that he endorsed this work. His approval meant everything.

A minute later, I made the call and left a message for Tessie. She called me back and, naturally, was surprised. She asked me to repeat myself when I said, "I am a medium who can help you with the lady spirit in your house."

She told me she would talk to her husband and get back to me.

I thought not too many partners would be open to this sort of thing and said to myself, "Well, that's the end of that—I made the call, and I am off the hook." I proclaimed to the Spirit World, "I kept my end of the bargain by calling her. Her husband is definitely not going to say yes."

To my amazement, Tessie called the next day and asked when I could come. I was astounded and yet slowly began to realize that the Spirit World was orchestrating all the arrangements. Tessie's husband was from Brazil. His grandmother could see Spirits, and he was familiar with spiritual things. I had made an incorrect assumption.

Next, I emailed my mentor to tell her about the house I intended to try to clear of unwanted spirits. She asked Archangel Michael and Saint John to accompany me to the house as extra protection. I was nervous but relieved to have two protectors from the Higher Realms. Since that time, both of these Masters have accompanied me to many of my house clearings. They are the ones who do the spiritual work, I am the conduit through which the Masters meet the spirits.

As I drove to the house, many things went through my head. I was very nervous about facing a spirit who had been murdered. What if I was unable to communicate with her? What if she ignored me? What if she would not leave? What about her husband? Was his spirit still there? I stood on the threshold before ringing their door-bell and closed my eyes. I could sense two very large angelic protectors flanking me. It felt as though a warm blanket enveloped me with fortification, and I relaxed. I knew I was completely protected and felt confident that the Spiritual Realm had my back!

As I stepped into the house, my Spirit Guide showed me images in my head of the crime that had taken place. Mark, the husband, stood in the upstairs hallway and commanded his wife to come upstairs. With the gun hidden from her sight, he waited for Jean to reach the top step. He shot her at close range, then instantly shot himself. I stood in the same upstairs hallway and sensed both Jean and Mark's spirits. I explained I was there to help them, not harm them.

Jean answered me, saying, "I was trying to protect the little girls from my husband." She thought he was going to harm the girls.

Mark's spirit felt shy and withdrawn, and Jean's spirit was the dominant personality wanting to protect. I explained to both spirits that they were dead and I was there to help them. I said my Spirit Guides and I wished to escort them to the other side where their friends and relatives would greet them. I could feel their relief when I explained, "I am not here to judge but only to assist you both to cross over." They believed me and agreed to accompany the Spirits and me to the entrance. I was relieved and elated. Jean's deceased mother greeted her, and Mark's brother was there for him. Jean and Mark had been stuck in their former home for more than four years; now, they were united with their deceased families on the Other Side.

Tessie and her family could resume their lives, no longer frightened by the "lady with the long hair." I called Tessie a week later to make sure the spirits were no longer in their house. She confirmed their two daughters were sleeping peacefully in their own bedroom, and her husband was no longer awakened in the middle of the night with a lady standing over him.

I was happy to tell my friend that my Spirit Guides and I had been successful in bringing both spirits to Heaven's threshold. She got upset with me and could not understand how I could bring the murdering, abusive husband to Heaven along with his wife, who was an innocent victim. I explained to her that it was not up to me to judge anyone. I am the glorified taxi driver. My mission is not to judge the deceased souls I meet but to assist them if I can.

When I was a teenager, my father would often remind me, "Tessie, don't judge; you're not dead yet!" How apropos, Pop! I smile now as I think of his words and try not to judge.

5

———

KATHY'S MOM

WORD SPREAD QUICKLY among my buddies that I could help ghosts. Another friend was worried about her deceased mother and asked me to stop by her mother's former house to see if I could sense her spirit inside the home.

My friend, Kathy, lived with her mother after her father passed. She took care of her mother until her mother passed, eight years after her father died. I had met Kathy's parents only a few times. After their mother passed, Kathy's siblings decided to rent the home instead of selling it. A young couple named Bill and Sally took the rental for a year.

Not long after they moved in, they began hearing and seeing a "lady" in spirit. One day Bill returned home from work. He told Kathy he distinctly heard a woman's voice call out, "Hello, hello, hello!" from Kathy's mother's first-floor bedroom. When he entered the bedroom, no one was there. Kathy explained that that was how her mother called out when anyone entered the house.

Another time, Sally and Bill entered the living room and saw a woman sitting on the couch in the exact spot where Kathy's mom used to sit. As they stood there looking at her, she faded until she disappeared before their eyes. They told Kathy that the woman looked like her but older! Kathy felt certain that Bill and Sally were seeing her mother, Betty. Kathy asked me to go to her mother's house to see if her mother was still there. She was worried and puzzled that her mother may have chosen to stay. Why hadn't she joined her father in Heaven?

I did not have access to the inside of her mother's rented house, which meant parking on the street in front of the property. I did not want to disappoint Kathy but did not know if I could help her mother. I was still new to this work and hoped my Spirit Guide would assist me. I tuned into the Spirit Realm and asked Spirit to be with me as I drove to Kathy's mom's house. I learned that I had to be able to turn it on and off, like a TV. As soon as I tuned in, a woman in spirit startled me as she sat next to me in my car. She was a petite lady with short blond hair, wearing a floral dress styled from the 1980s. She told me her name was Mary. I had never met Mary in person. She launched into her story and said that she was like a sister to Betty and had lived next door to her for twenty years. She and Betty had been extremely close friends, and she said Betty needed help. Mary knew Betty was in spirit and stuck on the fourth level. Mary also knew that Betty was afraid to go to the Other Side and confessed she never felt worthy or that she deserved to be with her beloved husband, Ben.

I parked my car in front of Betty's house. In order not to arouse suspicion from the neighbors, I pretended I was texting on my phone. I asked Betty, who was inside her house, to please come outside and talk to Mary and me. In an endearing voice, she called my name and got into my car. I felt grateful and happy that she would talk to me. I explained that I had this gift and could help her. Archangel St. Michael directed me to tell her she was deserving of her husband and true with a big heart. Mary told me she had been trying to convince Betty to go to her loving husband. Soon after, Betty believed us and was ready to join Ben. I was ecstatic when my Guide Michael, Mary, and I escorted her, and I watched them cross to the other side. It was a beautiful sight to see Ben waiting and greeting Betty with open arms. I could see his face was overjoyed and grateful to be reunited with her again in spirit.

Now I had a dilemma. Should I tell Kathy why her mother hadn't joined her father was because of unworthiness? I felt I was overstepping my bounds by telling Kathy her mother's deepest fear. What if Kathy had no knowledge about her mother's feelings of inadequacy? Kathy had never spoken to me about her mother in such a personal way. I felt I might betray an ethical trust for Kathy's opinion of her mother that I had no right to know. I wrestled with Spirit, then "heard" it was more important to tell her the truth, even if it cost me her friendship. Spirit said it was not up to me and my ego; I needed to tell Kathy what Mary told me. She had a right to know the reason why her mother had not gone to Heaven to be with her father. Feeling apprehensive, I told Kathy what Mary told me and was relieved by Kathy's reaction. She explained to me that Betty's father had verbally abused his daughter all her life. He belittled and maligned Betty, and she believed her father's words. Repeatedly, he told his daughter she was "stupid and no good and would never amount to anything." As a result, Betty never felt good enough. Even after her fifty-year marriage to Ben, she felt undeserving of him, yet she adored him, and he adored her. Kathy confirmed that what Mary told me was the truth about her mom. In addition, Kathy told me that Mary had been a confidant and best friend to Betty

Mary was a supportive angel who cared so much for her dear friend Betty that she came back to Earth from Heaven to help her cross over and be reunited with her beloved husband. What a true friend and love story! Love conquers all in this life and in the next.

This story taught me a valuable lesson to trust Spirit and give the message exactly as I hear it. Also, it validated that messages from Marys' spirit were all true and not fabricated by me. After that day, the rental couple never saw nor heard from Betty again.

One of the top three reasons the recently deceased do not automatically go to the Other Side is that they were told they were told and believed that they not worthy or good enough, that their life would never amount to anything, as in Betty's case.

As the Bible says, "For as a man thinketh in his heart, so he is." Unfortunately, Betty believed what her father repeatedly told her about herself—that she was no good. Most likely, her father was given that same message from his parents and possibly their parents before them, and so on. Betty broke that cycle by showing loving kindness to her children and everyone she met. It seems Betty never gave that love to herself while she was alive.

My heart goes out to those who never felt deserving of love for themselves. A high percentage of the spirits I meet unfortunately don't feel valuable or deserving within themselves to go to Heaven. It's important to know that we are all precious beings. We are all spiritual beings having an earthly experience. This place is Earth School, where we are here to experience this great place, but we forget who we really are—"beings of unconditional love and light" who did not originate on Earth but came from the Spirit World/ Heaven, where we will return after our lives here are finished.

Ghosts are afraid of being judged. People are afraid of being judged. Hell and Purgatory loom like a heavy cloud over the Catholic head, as well as over a lot of heads. But I think we are our own worst critics when it comes to judging ourselves. The thousands of ghosts I have witnessed walk happily over the threshold to their loved ones or pets in Heaven. They are overjoyed to be home.

When we die, our heart and soul—consciousness, emotions, memories, and personality—continue in a spirit form. Within that form, we retain everything that embodies the essence of who we really are. There is no death.

Think about your breath. You breathe in, and you breathe out your last physical breath, then you breath in again, and you are in the next realm. There is no break in the action of breathing. You may witness a person exhaling their last breath from their physical body, but what we do not see is them taking their next breath into their spiritual body. Our physical body is like a car, and you are the driver. The physical car may rust and disintegrate, but you continue in spirit form.

6

ENCOUNTERING WARRIORS IN BRAZIL

THERE ARE DIVERSE REASONS why the deceased may not go directly to Heaven. Spirits who die suddenly, whether on a battlefield or in a car accident, may not know they are dead and can remain stuck in the exact moment they died. If someone dies in January 1492, and I meet them in 2013, they are not a part of my time in the third dimension; they are stuck in their time of 1492 in the fourth dimension. Time stopped for them in 1492 when they passed from life into spirit. People who die on a battlefield can be stuck in that time and place fighting the same battle, sometimes for hundreds or even thousands of years. This is because, at the time of death, they lost the awareness of the progression of time. This occurs more often if the person is in a heightened emotional state when they pass over or if the death is unexpected and sudden. The next story is an illustration.

In December 2009, I travelled to Abadiânia, Brazil, to see a healer. The small country town is built atop crystal caves. Many spiritual healers and seekers from all over the world come to experience the otherworldly energy.

One afternoon, I sat on a bench atop a high plateau with a panoramic view of a huge field. I looked at the field far below me and was compelled to close my eyes. I opened myself to the Spiritual Realm and asked my Spirit Guide if there were any people on the land who needed assistance crossing over. Suddenly, my Spirit Guide switched on a movie in my head, and I was witnessing thousands of warriors from two ancient tribes battling with spears. The warriors were men clad in little more than a loin cloth but decorated with arm bands, anklets, and adornments in their long, dark hair. I remember the color red vividly standing out against their light brown skin. Their faces were painted, and the spears they were using were skillfully crafted and deadly.

The next thing I knew, I was in the middle of the huge field, walking in spirit form among them. Their long spears were piercing unfeeling through my spiritual body. The warriors were dumfounded as I kept walking and did not fall down dead. They dropped their spears, and looks of bewilderment replaced the anger that had existed moments before.

The fighting stopped, and the two tribes retreated to their separate sides of the field. With my intention to assist any spirits who needed help crossing over, I had pierced their time and must have materialized as an apparition.

The two tribal chiefs came into the middle of the field to speak to me. As I watched their spirits come toward me, I laughed to myself—that's what I do when I get nervous. Apparently, in spirit form, I maintain some of my human characteristics. What was I going to say to these guys, and how? What could the outcome possibly be? I didn't speak their language; I didn't even know what language they spoke. Furthermore, what did I look like? Was I still in my T-shirt and jeans? Was I now scantily clad in a period-appropriate loin cloth?

I heard a message loud and clear: "Spirit makes all the arrangements."

Feeling giddy, I knew I was here to do what I had offered myself up to Spirit to perform. I remembered the surrender of falling off my spiritual cliff and the affirmation it brought me. I took a deep breath and felt assured.

I began explaining, telepathically, that they were all dead and stuck in their time period on a battlefield, informing them it was now the twenty-first century and they were stuck in their century, which by appearances seemed a thousand years ago given their dress.

I asked, "Would you like to see a better way and go to a better place?" I only speak English, but they clearly understood the meaning of my words. This is where Spirit must have interpreted whatever I was thinking to make sure it got across to them. It was my turn to be shocked, for both sides agreed to go with me.

When I asked them all to line up behind me, people began to materialize out of the trees lining either side of the battlefield. They lined up by rank: the old men were first, then the chiefs, the warriors next, then young boys, then the old women, mothers, and young girls with babies. At the entrance to the gateway, I stepped to one side and watched thousands of people reverently enter through the simple doorway to the other side. I could feel the humility and willingness of the entire group. There was an overwhelming sense of "oneness" and unity in tribes that, up until moments before, had been warring for centuries. They did not glance back at me as many spirits had. They acted quietly and diminutively as they walked inside. I don't know what nirvana looked like for this particular culture or if they had ever thought about life after death. I do know that they came with me because Spirit could communicate through me that something more was awaiting them.

I can only wonder at the mystical machinations behind the scenes in the Spirit Realm. My Spirit Guide explained that through my intention of wanting to help, a connection with willing souls who are inclined to progress is made. I try to assure the souls that the next place is benevolent, positive, and loving. They have to be willing to go, and they have a choice. I can only assist them if they are inclined to proceed. The Spiritual Realm orchestrates the details.

The tribes had such a strong sense of purpose fighting for their own side and the lives of their families. It was those strong emotions that kept them stuck fighting in that time for so long. Our emotions can overtake our real selves and our reasoning. Personalities remain intact after we die, as our "real selves" are not our physical bodies. Dying with our emotions having gotten the better of us can keep us stuck until someone or something outside of ourselves interjects to break the cycle. Maintaining emotional balance and equilibrium during life helps influence what happens to our spirit when we die. Anger, hate, and fighting on the negative end of the scale must be balanced by joy, happiness, laughter, and love. The positive end of the scale can outrank the negative, but it takes being aware of each feeling we allow to take up space in our hearts and minds. It's so important to be joyous—just as the unseen wind tickles the trees into laughter, unseen emotions affect us. Bringing awareness to the emotions we perpetuate and consciously choosing joy impacts not only the moment we are in but also the time our souls will occupy.

It was amazing to me the warriors were unable to awaken to the fact that they had all perished a long time ago. It took an interruption in their intense emotional routine of fighting for them to become aware. My willingness to reach across the ethers into their space and time was enough to surprise them into putting down their spears and wondering what was happening. The Spirit Realm mysteriously worked with me, and together we helped these lost souls move on to a higher dimension.

BRAZILIAN WARRIORS' LIMERICK

The Chirps and the Chires
Were there in shire
When next to the fire I came

I had heard their fine "singing"
My ears they were ringing
And I joined them to do just the same

I offered them heaven
On the day of the seven
And they lined up in order of rank

They trudged close behind me
Their odor did find me
And Lawdy did some of them stank

Through the gates every brave
Left with nary a wave
I was glad they had all ceased their fight

My job was complete
Their spirits, replete
And I turned 'round and called it a night

Your mind has the power
At your final hour
And so you must focus on good

Make a hell out of heaven
Or a heav'n of hell
Only you can make this understood

—*Kathryn L. Michelotti*

7

———————

SAM'S FATHER

OFTEN, I AM ASKED what happens to the spirits I meet who do not want to move on? The answer is the spirits remain where they want to be in the fourth dimension around the Earth plane. I cannot force a spirit to progress unless it is their idea to do so; I can merely extend the offer to help them. I've met many spirits who were not ready and had no intention of moving to the Other Side. A compelling reason to stay, or haunt, is determined by a spirit's emotional experience during their life time. A spirit desires to go where they felt and enjoyed an intense emotional attachment. There are as many reasons to remain here as there are numbers of people, and some have made their intention very clear to me that they are staying put. Some fear the judgement of "hell," or their lives on earth are familiar. A really big one is they are afraid of the unknown, or they feel unworthy, or they don't want to leave their loved ones, beloved places, or prized possessions, or they have unfinished business. Some do not want to leave their earthly addictions to alcohol or drugs.

This next story is a prime example of a spirit refusing to budge from the Earth plane.

My friend Sam thought the spirits of his deceased father and sister were occupying the house where they were raised. Sam's father had died about ten years prior, but his sister had recently died of breast cancer. Their father was overbearing, and Sam feared his sister was being held there by him. Their childhood had been highly emotionally charged because of their abusive, alcoholic father.

Sam's family had not lived in the house for many years. I have noticed that many spirits return to places where they grew up because it is familiar and filled with emotional energy. Sam asked me to drive to the house to see if they were "haunting" there. I had never met Sam's father or sister when they were alive. As I drove to his former house, I opened up to my Spirit Guide and "tuned in." I did not know what to expect but trusted the Spirit World to inform me.

The dirt driveway had a small space for me to turn my car around without being seen by the current occupants. As I sat in my car (pretending to be on my phone), I could "see" the spirit of Sam's father glaring at me through the kitchen window. I could hear him exclaiming about the new liquor store down the street and how excited he was and could visit anytime. He was jonesing for some hard liquor. I told him I wanted to help him to the Other Side and asked if he would like to go with me. He interrupted and declared he was not going anywhere. Then he glanced at a woman cowering in the corner and said in a menacing voice, "And she's not going anywhere either."

Her spirit was so meek, and he tried to stop me from talking to her, but I ignored him and addressed her directly. I said, "I realize you love your father, and you're in a difficult position to even acknowledge what I am saying, but I hope you value yourself enough to stand up for yourself one day. You have free will, and you have a new spiritual life now that you can use to continue to grow.

There is more to your spiritual life than this. I know it's too hard to contemplate now, but one day, when you are ready, I'll be here to help you move to a better place—Heaven."

She did not (or could) not respond to me. I could feel her personality so indicative of a child of an abusive alcoholic. You almost do not possess your own personality and become an extension of the abuser. Her father did not want to be alone and was unwilling to let her go. She needed an outside influence, an interruption to her intense emotional situation. But fear is a strong inhibitor. I interjected and broke the cycle of fighting in Brazil, and I tried to interject in this cycle of abuse to give Sam's sister a glimpse of another, better way. Except, at this time, she was not ready, so it did not work. She was exercising her "free will."

Alive or in spirit, we do not always realize that we possess the key to unlocking ourselves from any uncomfortable situation. Empowerment lies within us, but often we need to be reminded of that by someone other than ourselves. To have faith that there exists another way, a higher power, or loving guidance that wants us to be happy and live our best life and spiritual life. It's imperative to block out the outside influence of the negative and fire up the Divine spark within.

I told Sam what happened. He was disappointed and sad for his sister. He said that when his father was alive, he was a terrible alcoholic. He was not surprised that his father chose to remain in his former home. It was hard for me to explain to my friend there was nothing more I could say or do until one or both of them decided they were ready to move on. I told Sam to pray for them

Sam's father didn't want to leave the Earth plane because of his strong emotional attachment to what he loved most in life—booze. Many spirits I've met remain here for years because of their strong emotional attachments to things. Wherever they felt their strongest emotions is where they want to be; it is an addiction.

Many spirits believe that the life they experienced here is all there is. They mistakenly believe there is nothing else after their physical life.

Instead of moving on, the spirits go to the places they enjoyed and loved when they were alive. Those places can be a "home" for centuries. Perhaps, after a while, they tire of it and wonder if there is something else. Sometimes the wondering is enough of an interruption to the emotional cycle to trigger a desire to move on. When a lost spirit exercises free will and wants to leave the Earth plane, the Higher Spirits hear their call. We all have free will, and we each decide when to advance to a higher level. That's when someone like me can help. I tune into the Spirit World and ask if anyone needs my assistance. When our spirit does arrive in Heaven, the opportunity is present for furthering our spiritual advancing. Each and every one of us deserves to go to Heaven.

As human beings, emotions and emotional attachments can over power and rule us if we allow them. Strong emotions can drive obsessions that alter us to become out of balance. Jealousy and pain can dictate our behavior. Anger is a strong emotion; like attracts like.

As I mentioned before, the deceased spirit does not progress in our time. Whatever day, time, hour they die, freezes at their second of death. Nor do they feel anything at the second of death where time does not progress linearly.

8

―――――

TED

T HE SPIRITUAL WORLD does have a sense of humor. One Sunday morning in spring, I was enjoying a drive through Vermont, listening to music and daydreaming. Suddenly, I was jolted out of my reverie by a ghost who fell through the roof of my car and settled onto my passenger seat. A second before he arrived, I had driven past the exit where my sister-in-law, Pam, lived. I was reminiscing how her brother, Ted, had died of a heart attack the previous spring while skiing with his daughter. Out of nowhere, with no warning, Ted in spirit, had appeared next to me. He did not acknowledge me; he just stared straight ahead.

I thought, *Is this really happening? Is Pam's deceased brother really sitting in the front seat of my car, or is this my imagination?* I had not seen Ted in thirty years; this guy was in his late sixties, with scraggly white hair, but his facial features seemed similar to Ted's. I asked my Spirit Guide what the heck was happening. Then my Spirit Guide switched on a scene in my head of how and where Ted had passed. It was a sunny, clear-blue-sky day, and snow conditions were perfect for a day on the slopes. Ted and his daughter were standing side by side at the top of a mountain. She began to ski down the slope but soon stopped when she realized her father had not joined her. She turned around in time to see him simply fall forward head first into the snow.

I wondered why Ted was not trying to talk or look at me; I was unsure if he was next to me in spirit or my imagination. I asked my Guide for a sign, and in the next instant, I drove over a bridge named "Wilson." Wilson was Pam and Ted's other brother. It was a coincidence to see the name Wilson at the exact second I asked for a sign. In addition, I felt a calm feeling that simply rang true in my heart. I thanked my Spirit Guide for the signs. I then knew that Ted's spirit really was in the passenger seat, and I was not imagining it!

Telepathically, I said, "Hi, Ted."

Now it was his turn to be shocked. He turned to me and said, "You can see and hear me?"

I answered, "Yes, I can hear you, see you, and communicate telepathically with you."

He was astounded. "Neat parlor trick," he said. When he answered, I could hear it in my head. (This is why, in the early stages of having this "spiritual gift," I thought I might be crazy by hearing voices.) Using telepathy, I explained that I could help him, that I was a medium with an ability to forge a connection between this world and the next.

Ted and I grew up in the same village. I looked up to him as he was my eldest brother's friend and brother-in-law. It was exciting for me to communicate with him on this very different level. I was still new at this and unsure of his impression of me, the "kid sister." He was as surprised to be in my car as I was to have him there.

He said that he did not know how he got into my car. He didn't know what was expected of him and added that he had no idea where he was; he felt lost.

I explained that he had passed away suddenly on the ski slope while skiing with his daughter. I let him know that, with the assistance of my Spirit Guide, I could escort him to Heaven if he was willing to go. He revealed to me that he did not feel worthy or deserving to be in Heaven. Ted's spirit told me he was afraid of being judged since he felt his life was not lived as an exemplary Catholic. We are our own worst critics.

I tried to assure him he was a worthy spiritual being and the Spiritual World would gladly welcome him home. I requested my Spirit Guide to please bring loving family members in spirit to encourage him.

The next thing I saw was Ted's father on the threshold of Heaven, waiting to greet Ted and help him cross to the Other Side. Although Ted was only nine years old when his father passed, they had been very close, and Ted missed him terribly all his life. They were so happy to see each other again, and Ted sprinted across the threshold into his father's arms. I could see they loved and missed each other very much. Before they walked away, they turned to wave good bye to me. I am filled with immense gratitude to witness these beautiful reunions. I love my job!

People who appear to welcome new spirits home have had strong emotional ties with them in life. I have seen parents and grandparents come through, friends and first crushes. I have even seen pets anyone the spirit had a deep love for. When the spirits are lost and confused, they are looking for safety and security. It's another piece of our human personalities that persists beyond our bodies. Seeing a loved one returns one's emotional state to joy and sets the stage for a fruitful spiritual life.

The rest of the car ride was quiet that morning. I was happy for Ted and relieved he was no longer lost and afraid but happily reunited with his father in Heaven. I thanked my Spiritual Guide once again for proof of the "sign" I needed. With each spiritual incident, I felt more comfortable doing this new "job." It occurred to me that I was "on call" whenever the Spiritual Realm and my Spirit Guide needed me to assist with a soul or souls. I was beginning to feel okay with it, even though it startled me in my car!

The difference between me asking if I can help and suddenly being confronted with a spirit was something I had to get used to. I never knew when a spirit would be brought to me. My Spirit Guides are like otherworldly mentors who know my strengths, know when I'm tired, know when it's best to nudge me into closing my eyes or when to drop a spirit into my proverbial lap. I marvel at how well this ability flows with my life. While I never know what to expect, I am secure in the knowledge that it always works.

I can't think of a time when I was inconvenienced by my new calling. Except once when I was at a wake with my mother. You'll remember, dear reader, that my mother was one of the greatest spiritual-lesson bringers in my life, and she was not an easy grader; rarely did I achieve higher than a D. But I digress. I was kneeling at the casket of a childhood friend, and I felt this rain of energetic fuzz envelop me while Spirit said, "You need to bring her up now."

My mother was next to me, deep in prayer. As I began to bring the woman up, my mother elbowed me sharply in the ribs, jolting me out of the process. You see, I was praying for too long, in her estimation. Guess I got a "D" in how to attend a wake too. Imagine her horror if she had known what I was truly doing and to whom I was speaking. Later, I talked to the woman's spirit and brought her to heaven. It was so unexpected to be called to bring her up right then and there, especially with my spiritually challenging mother present. Spirit and I have stronger boundaries now, where I feel comfortable saying, "Not right now."

9

———

THE STEPMOTHER

MARSHALL WAS HAVING TROUBLE with a "ghost" in his house. Marshall said most days his morning coffee mug would be knocked off the counter and onto the kitchen floor. Household items, such as car keys, would go missing. Sometimes, late at night, he could hear a woman's voice calling out in the unused bedroom down the hall, and a picture frame would be on the floor. It sounded like Marshall had a poltergeist. He lived in a large house with his longtime partner, who did not believe in ghosts. The night before I went to their house, "someone" knocked loudly several times on their front door. When Marshall opened the door, no one was there. I sensed that the spirit was trying to scare them and perhaps keep me from coming.

As I drove to Marshall's home the next day, I tuned into Spirit. Nothing. There was no information about what was happening in the house. They were not telling me anything about the ghost ahead of time. I walked through the house with Marshall, starting in the attic and going into all of the rooms. In each room, I tuned into Spirit and asked if anyone needed my help. There was no reply, and I was beginning to feel confused.

As we descended the basement stairs, I encountered my first spirit, but it was't human! The spirit of a sweet black lab was curled up under the stairs. When I described the dog to Marshall, he was delighted that his beloved Bailey was around. When Bailey was alive, his favorite place to sleep was curled up under the basement stairs! Marshall grew sad as he reminisced about his pup. A truly great dog comes along once in a lifetime, and Bailey had been Marshall's best friend. When he had died a few years earlier, Marshall was devastated. While seeing beautiful reunions is one of the great parts of what I do, I also treasure the bittersweet stories of love that people share with me. Everyone has lost someone precious, and I hold that in my consciousness to be gentle with the people I meet.

I soon noticed someone else in the basement; this time, the spirit was human. A woman was cowering in the corner and trying to hide from me.

The first thing I told her was, "I am not going to hurt you; I am here to help you."

My Spirit Guide told me that whenever Marshall went into the basement, his faithful dog would stand up, growl, and bark at the lady spirit. That was why Bailey slept under the basement stairs when he was alive and why he remained there still. Bailey had always been there to protect Marshall from her. It was then that Marshall gave me the background of the previous owner of the house.

Fifteen years ago, Marshall had purchased this house from Rob. Rob had grown up in the house with his father and stepmother, his biological mother having died when he was very young. Rob's father travelled extensively and was rarely home. This left Rob alone with his stepmother for weeks at a time. When Rob was a boy in the

1950s, his stepmother would physically torture him in the basement. The father never knew what went on there when he was absent. I told Spirit not to show me what happened or describe the sordid details of the torture. The pain humans inflict on one another is not something I handle well emotionally, nor is it necessary to know details. My purpose is to help spirits move on from the Earth plane, regardless of how or why they have become stuck. I felt the step mother was remorseful for mistreating Rob for years in that basement. She kept telling me how sorry she was and that she regretted torturing him. She said when she was a child, her mother had abused her, and as a result she, in turn, had inflicted pain upon her stepson.

I have seen this often with spirits and in life. Many people come from families with a history of abuse. If one person can do the work on themselves to heal that generational pain, they can break the cycle. It is hard work to face one's demons, but the restorative effects go back to the spirits who have come before and continue far into future generations.

This spirit was terrified that I was going to judge and condemn her. I informed her it was not my business to judge; I was only there to escort her to Heaven if she was willing to go. It took a while to convince her I was there to help her move on to a better place. I told her I believed we were all spiritual beings having an earthly experience. I explained she had to work on improving herself on the Other Side to strive toward being a kinder soul. After a while, she felt prepared to go and see what awaited her. I asked the Spiritual Realm to bring a family member or friend to meet her and help her cross. She was surprised and glad to see her mother and grandmother waiting for her. I watched the three women embrace for a long time and then disappear.

I then turned to Bailey and asked him if he wanted to go to the Other Side. It still baffles me how the dog understood what I was saying. I also wonder what Bailey's idea of the Other Side was. This is another marvel of how Spirit works with all the creatures in our world. Bailey was not inclined to budge from under the stairs, and despite the lady spirit being gone, he seemed content to remain with Marshall. Bailey showed me that Marshall had meant just as much to him and was also his "best friend."

You may wonder how I could help the spirit of a person who tortured an innocent child. My responsibility is to remain emotionally neutral and escort all deceased spirits from the Earth plane to the threshold of Heaven, providing they are willing to go. As I mentioned, my role is not to judge but simply guide them home. I must admit, staying neutral where children are concerned is challenging, but it is not about me; it is about the spirits I am there to assist.

IO

WOMAN ON A CARIBBEAN BEACH

Whenever I meet a recently deceased spirit, I have a special role to fill. Often they are confused and may not know what happened or where they are. I inform them gently that they have died, and I explain I am there to help them to the Other Side if they are ready to go. If they have died on the day I happen to meet them, I explain they have three days to visit their loved ones and say their goodbyes. Even though the living may not hear them, it gives closure to the recently deceased. I ask them to return to me in three days at the exact spot where we first met. Then I can take them to the Other Side.

I have had the privilege of helping deceased people from many cultures. It makes no difference what beliefs they espoused when they were alive. We are all spiritual beings returning home to the source of all. Thus far, all the spirits have returned to me within three days to be escorted to the Other Side. When I meet spirits who have been stuck in their time period for weeks, years, or even centuries, I can cross them over immediately if they choose to go. An example of a spirit returning to me after three days is illustrated in this next story.

I do not know what to expect from the Spirit Realm nor when I will be needed. My husband and I were in the Caribbean for the winter months, and every morning we took a walk on the beach. It's a lovely two-mile stretch that we enjoy while holding hands and keeping our feet in the surf. One sunny morning, we witnessed paramedics trying to revive a woman lying lifeless on a lounge chair. They worked vigorously, pumping on her chest, attempting to resuscitate her. Suddenly my Spirit Guide explained to me that she was gone. She had been swimming in the ocean, had a heart attack in the rough waves, and drowned. I saw her spirit standing near her body, looking dazed and confused. I noticed a paramedic writing down her time of death, and I heard her mention the woman was fifty-eight years old. I began talking to her spirit telepathically and asked her name. She acted startled when she heard me and told me her name was Diane. I calmly informed her that she had passed while swimming. Diane was shocked by the news and did not believe me initially. My Spirit Guide let me know she was an American. Gently, I asked her to go back home to the States to visit her family, pets, and friends and say goodbye to them. Although her loved ones might not be able to hear her, I knew it would give her some peace. Then I asked her to return in three days to the same place on the beach.

Diane's husband had accompanied her to the beach that day. They were on a much-needed vacation and had been thoroughly enjoying themselves. My Guide told me he had had too much to drink and passed out on another lounge chair nearby. He was unaware of what had happened to his wife. Can you imagine the shock he must have had when he awoke to find his wife gone? I remember seeing the paramedics trying to wake him up, but he was sound asleep. Diane was standing near him, trying to communicate with him, but it was no use.

Three days later, I saw Diane's spirit standing anxiously in the same spot on the beach. She was alternating between looking out over the waves and glancing back at the lounge chairs. I caught her glancing upward with an unsure look upon her face. Her anxiety was spiritually palpable. As I approached her, I asked my Spirit Guide to please bring a family member from the Other Side to help ease her transition. Her deceased mother showed up and was waiting for her on the Other Side. When Diane saw her mother waving at her, her entire demeanor changed. Her face lit up into a beaming smile. Diane said she and her mother had been very close in life. She shared with me that she had been depressed and missed her mother more than anyone in the world since she had passed away five years ago. She eagerly and confidently crossed over to her.

Could this woman who died so suddenly on an island beach have gone to the Other Side on her own? My sense is that it may have taken her a long time because she was disoriented, confused, shocked, and unaware that she had passed. Additionally, her anxiety at what was to come next may have prevented her from taking the next steps alone.

My role in this is to put my trust in Spirit at any time and be ready and trust that when they alert me of a situation, I respond and help. They do not ask me in words; they merely indicate with an awareness of a situation. They do not interfere with "free will," mine or anyone else's.

When my Spirit Guide showed me a person standing near her drowned body and explained how she died, I knew I needed to help her. It is never up to me to decide when someone is ready to go. Diane was willing because she wanted to be wherever her mother was. I watched the pair hug as though they would never let go of each other again.

I feel honored and privileged to help spirits to the next level of their spiritual journey. However, it was upsetting to witness someone's final moments. So precious is life, and in a blink, it is finished. It is my understanding that at the second before impending death, angels whisk our spirit out of our bodies. This applies to anyone who dies from an illness, in a coma, in a car accident, fighting armies, drowning, or murder, to name a few. We may not feel the exact second of transition, which may explain why people may not realize they are dead or what has happened to them or where they are. I've heard it described as taking a breath here, then taking the next breath there.

I often think of Diane's' husband waking up to find his wife deceased. Many a time, I have wished there was a way I could bring as much comfort to the living as I see in the spirits I help. On the positive side, what a way to leave this Earth—swimming in the crystal waves of the Caribbean on a warm, sunny beach in January.

* * *

I am often asked if I am afraid of ghosts. I figure they are dead and cannot hurt me—besides, I immediately tell them I want to help. Fortunately, I am not afraid because of the confidence, reliance, and knowing that Spirit has my back. Spirit has your back too! We can all believe they have our backs. Just because we cannot see them with our physical eyes, it does not mean they are not there. We have God-given "free will" to choose to do what we want. A blessing if we use it wisely and a curse if we do not. We do not walk through this life alone. We have help standing by us, waiting to be asked.

I have empathy for the ghosts because they were people like you and me who passed and are now disoriented. They know people can't hear, see, or touch them, but they are not at rest either. The spirits I meet are usually lost, confused, and unaware of what exactly happened to them. These ghosts will seek out living people who are clairvoyant, clairsentient, or clairaudient, like me, in an attempt to understand their current situation. For these spirits, their experience is very much like Bruce Willis's character in *The Sixth Sense*. He can tell something is off with his "life," but he does not realize he is deceased until he is ready to acknowledge it from someone he can communicate with. I am not afraid of ghosts because of the protection and guidance I ask for and feel from the Divine Spirit World. My strong desire to help spirits is conveyed to them, and they become receptive and willing.

II

THE THREE TWENTY-NINE
YEAR OLDS

T HAT IS NOT TO SAY that my work is completely void of fear. I had a terrifying experience in February of 2011. My Guide gave me explicit news that in the upcoming spring, I would be bringing three twenty-nine-year-old men to the Other Side. My Guide also mentioned that all three young men were still alive! Instantly, I was an emotional wreck because my own son was twenty-nine years old at the time! I panicked at the thought of losing him. It would have been too horrific and cruel to imagine that the Spirit Realm would ask me to bring my own son to the Other Side.

I asked my Guide if my son was going to die, and there was no reply. Anxiously and selfishly, I waited and prayed that my son would not be among the three young men. A part of me hoped that perhaps I was imagining I had heard this news, but deep down, I knew better than not to trust my intuition and Spirit Guide. My ability to discern the difference between my Guide's voice and my own internal dialogue has become proficient. I told no one this disturbing news, and I tried not to think about what would happen in the coming season. It was difficult waiting for something of this magnitude to happen to these boys—and my involvement.

In mid-March, the first young man passed. My daughter in New Hampshire called me in Connecticut to tell me her best friend's brother had crashed his car head-on into a tree. Instantly, my Guide showed me a movie of what had happened. Nick was looking down on the passenger-side floor for a dropped CD when the car swerved and lost control. My Guide said he did not feel the impact from hitting the tree as angels whisked his spirit out of his body right before impact.

As Kate was telling me about Nick, suddenly his spirit was with us on the telephone. Using mental telepathy that only I could hear, he said, "Who the f— are you?"

I told my daughter that Nick was on the phone with us. I had never met Nick in person, but my daughter knew him and his family. I sensed his energy; he was angry, agitated, and trying not to let me know he was scared. He said he had no clue where he was or what had happened to him. I felt sorry for him and tried to calm him down. I explained I was Kate's mom and could help him cross over to Heaven. I told him his body had died when his car hit a tree and that his spirit was in-between worlds. Nick's energy calmed down considerably when he realized he could communicate with someone. It was important to him that I understood he had not meant to die when he tried to grab the CD off the floor of his car. It was truly an accident that happened in a split second when he lost control of the car. The accident occurred on a beautiful clear Colorado day in mid-afternoon while doing something ordinary. How many times have we all reached for something while driving? But when our time is up in this life, it is up. I asked him to go say his goodbyes to his parents and sister, then return to me in three days, and I would help him.

Three days later, Nick came to see me. He had been happy with his life and was disappointed that his time on Earth was over. He had so much to live for: he was excited about a new job and had just built a house for himself.

He said he would miss his family most of all. He visited his relatives and friends in those three days and said what he wanted, even though they could not hear him. He also attended his own celebration of life and was elated by the overwhelming sentiments shared around a bonfire. He had even accompanied my daughter when she retrieved his belongings from his car. As she picked up his CD wallet, she noticed one was missing—the one he had tried to pick up from the floor before he crashed.

Nick told me he was upset to think that some people thought perhaps he committed suicide. He pleaded with me to tell his mother he did not commit suicide—it was a stupid mistake.

When he was ready to go with my Spirit Guide and me, he was relaxed and not anxious or fearful of the unknown. I witnessed his grandparents there to greet him and watched him walk calmly to them. Nick seemed ready, content, and at peace.

In April, I met the second twenty-nine-year-old spirit who passed. My brother called me to say one of our friends from childhood had lost a son. I had never met the son, but my family had been close with the father, Joe, who had become a hard-working doctor driven by a strict and disciplined work ethic. His son, Stan, had apparently committed suicide by carbon monoxide poisoning, sitting in his car in his garage with the motor running.

As I stood outside the funeral home, waiting to go inside to pay my respects to Stan at his wake, I sensed his presence and began communicating with him telepathically. I told him I'd gone to Grammar School with his dad, Joe. Stan told me he had ADHD and explained he could no longer cope with his life. My Guide told me it was difficult for his father's ego to accept a son with ADHD—his son's condition did not jive with Joe's high expectations. Stan pushed himself academically all his life and graduated from a prestigious college in New Hampshire. Dealing with ADHD was no easy feat for Stan, but he wanted to accomplish the degree for his father. He told me he never felt desired or valued by his father. He loved him, but he felt defeated and was tired of trying to please him. In addition, the medication he took for ADHD left him conflicted and confused.

Even though Stan knew what he was doing as he sat in his car in his garage, he said he did not think he would really die. "It was a cry for help, and I hoped I would be saved at the last moment," he said. Sadly, that moment never arrived.

After he got all this off his chest, Stan felt I understood his situation, and we went together to the gateway to Heaven. His grandparents were there to greet him with open arms, and Stan ran to meet them.

As tragic as this story is for the living, my role is to help the spirits. I do not usually share the details with the family unless they show me they are open to hearing them. Sharing Stan's feelings with Joe would only serve to hurt Joe for the remainder of his life here on Earth without his son. Stan, however, was no longer stuck, and with his heavy burden unloaded onto me, he felt lighter and freer than he had ever known. He could move on with no hard feelings.

When May arrived, I met the third young man in spirit. I was attending a church funeral for an old family friend, Mr. Purnell, when suddenly, in the pew next to me was his grandson, Sean, in spirit. I had never met Sean in life, but he seemed disoriented and confused. He didn't know where he was—only that he was in church. Sean had followed his entire family to his grandfather's funeral. I explained I was a friend of his family and that I could help him. He told me the last thing he remembered was partying and drinking with his friends a week ago on a Saturday night. After the party, he'd gone home and passed out. What Sean did not know was he had not awakened the next morning. My Guide told me Sean had died of alcohol poisoning. I explained to Sean that he was dead and I could help him to the entrance of Heaven. While sitting in the pew at his grandfather's funeral, my Guide and I brought Sean to the Other Side. He was delighted to see his grandfather on the other side, already waiting for him. The two men smiled, then turned and looked over their shoulders at me and waved goodbye. Sean and his grandfather had both passed away on the same day—Father's Day!

I have to confess the joy, relief, and guilt I felt that my son was not one of the three twenty-nine-year olds to die that spring. I was fearful that my Guides would ask this of me, but looking back now, I realize my Guides knew me and my limitations and would not ask me to do that.

This experience brought up so many questions that I do not have the answers to. How did Spirit know ahead of time those three boys, who were alive in February, would all pass that spring? Do our souls plan our lives before we are born, as the Akashic Records indicate? Nick, Stan, and Sean were all twenty-nine years old, and all three passed in three consecutive spring months, just as my Spirit Guide foretold. To my knowledge, their paths had never crossed in life, and they never knew one another. I had never met any of the young men while they were alive, yet I was connected to all three through friends of my family, and that connection is what enabled me to help each of them.

Are our lives predestined? Is everything we do preordained? Is all the world a stage, as Shakespeare said, and we are acting out a play that we think is not foretold? We do have free will—our God-given right. God and the Spirit world cannot intervene with our free will. The Akashic Records say everything past, present, and future about our lives is contained in those records. Are we all just actors following a script already known to the higher realms? It would appear to be true in this case. It seems our lives truly are playing out a predetermined mystery. Without a playbook, we can only try our best on this stage called life.

12

THE GRAND DAME
OF THE TOWN

OUR REAL SELF CONTINUES to exist in a spiritual form after our bodies cease. Our body is the car, and we are the driver; the driver is the Real Self. The car or body dies, but not the driver or soul. Personalities, dreams, experiences, and thoughts are contained in our soul or Real Self and remain intact. Some of the most fun I have had with spirits is when they have strong personalities undiminished by the lack of a corporeal body. They still command the same respect and authority they demanded in life. This next story is about such a woman.

A friend of mine, Ingrid, asked me to clear the house she was moving into. Negative energy from previous residents (including her fiancé's ex) had built up over time, and my friend was sensitive enough to feel it impacting her enjoyment of her new home.

As I drove to the house, I opened up to my Spirit Guide to get an idea of the circumstances surrounding the house. Suddenly, I distinctly heard a woman say, "A lady wears her hair up!" The imperious tone was admonishing and commanding, as if the speaker would have nothing to do with me until I complied.

I pulled my car over as I smiled to myself and immediately put my hair on top of my head with a clip. I have found it prudent to comply with the spirit's wishes if the request is within reason. When I arrived at the house, I discovered a formidable "grand dame" sitting on the apex of the high roof. She was accompanied by an entourage of family members in spirit: her young granddaughter of about eighteen, a grand-nephew of twenty-five years, and her two sons in their forties. My Spirit Guide informed me she always had an entourage of admirers in life. I waited patiently outside her estate to speak with the former "Lady of the House." After a while, she deigned to speak to me. The grand dame's spirit wanted there to be no doubt in my mind as to who she was—the most influential lady of her day in town! She had given lavish balls for the most prominent people, and she was appalled that her favorite room for entertaining had been turned into "that lawyer's office!" The Grand Dame told me she did not care for the present tenant, Ingrid's fiancé, a lawyer. Despite the fact that he had lived there for over thirty years, she thought him a scoundrel and did not like or approve of him! However, she liked my friend, Ingrid, very much and hoped she would take her place as the dignified "Lady of the House."

Then Spirit showed me a movie of what the house looked like in the Grand Dame's day (circa 1920s). Chauffeurs drove luxury cars to the front door with a butler in attendance to open doors for guests as they arrived. Only the high society of the town—the "captains of industry" of the time—were invited to her very social parties. To be invited meant you would further your social standing and career. She was the modern-day equivalent of an "influencer," and she took her role very seriously.

I could see her quiet, cajoling husband at Heaven's gate, waiting ever patiently for her to cross over to him. She had been dead at least sixty years, but she never wanted to leave her home until she felt it was in the right hands. It was important to her that I tell Ingrid to please live in the house after her and take her place as lady of the house!

I cleared the negative energy inside the house and relayed the sentiments to Ingrid. Only then did the Grand Dame agree to go with my Spirit Guide and me to the Other Side. She was especially pleased when she saw her patient husband waiting for her. They loved each other, and it was apparent she "wore the pants in the family." The other relatives in her entourage followed her. I think they had been with her on the roof to try to convince her to go with me; they seemed to genuinely love and care for her. The Grand Dame needed and wanted to tell her story one last time. Additionally, she wanted to ensure a "proper lady" would take her place and not that horrible woman who had lived with the lawyer for twenty years! She had relished her role in life as a dominant woman in high society and carried that charisma into her afterlife. Upon death, we do not necessarily become benign angels floating on clouds for all eternity. How boring would that be?

Spirits love to tell me their stories. I think that is one of my favorite "perks," if you will. Imagine sitting with an ancestor and hearing firsthand their experiences of a time long forgotten. The world and its inhabitants were so different then. It almost seems a fiction, but it is not; it's the reality of the spirits I encounter. That reality is so important for them to retell because passing on their story keeps them alive in a way. I get a glimpse of history each time I encounter a stuck spirit, and I am so grateful.

I3

THE ILL-FATED COUPLE

L OVE NEVER DIES. Love lives on in our hearts forever, even after death. Just as our personalities are not confined to our corporeal experiences, neither is our love. This next story is an illustration of love so strong and deep it is not broken in death, even if murder is involved!

Joanne and Ed owned a stately mansion built in 1910. In the side yard stood an old sunken rose garden with a large fountain in the center. Joanne called me to say she had seen a few of her deceased family members sitting on top of the west wall of the garden. While Joanne could feel that her family members were at peace, she was curious to see if they would speak to her through me. Joanne and Ed asked me to come and take a look and see if I could help. I am never sure what to expect, but I trust my Spirit Guide will show me where I am needed.

In this instance, instead of being a medium between Joanne and her ancestors, my Guide showed me a scene of completely unrelated events. The experience was like a movie turning on in my mind. The first thing Spirit showed me was a large, extravagant party in progress inside the house. It was the 1920s, and people were elegantly dressed in the attire of that time. The next scene I witnessed took place outside in the dark shadows of the sunken rose garden between two party guests. A couple were arguing in the far corner of the garden. A beautiful young woman was dressed in a long slim white satin dress. Her blond hair was exquisitely held together on top of her head by diamond-studded combs. The handsome young man was in a tuxedo. They were quarreling loudly as she told him she was pregnant and demanded he divorce his wife and marry her. The gentleman was a wealthy businessman who was prominent in the community. He told her he could not afford to lose his social standing as it was his wife's family money and his wife would ruin him.

In the next instant, Spirit showed me how he lost control of himself, put his hands around her throat, and strangled her in the heat of passion in that corner of the garden. He then ran to his chauffeur, who was waiting by his car. The chauffeur helped him put her lifeless body into the trunk of the large car. Together they drove her body a few miles away and dumped her into Long Island Sound. No one ever knew nor discovered that he had gotten away with murder.

The young murderer never got over his love for the young woman he killed. When I met the couple in spirit, they were shyly standing close together, side-by-side in the garden in the same place where he had killed her. It was clear to me they still loved each other very much. After his earthly life ended, he returned to the garden where he had killed her and never left her side. They were two spirits in love in the garden and had remained there for over eighty years. The young woman never wanted to leave the garden, even after he murdered her, and the remorseful lover always wanted to be with her. It was also the last place they had been alive together, and neither was willing to leave without the other.

Joanne's ancestors played an important role in helping this couple. They showed themselves to Joanne, and this alerted her. She, in turn, called me so I could help them. When I went into the garden, Joanne's ancestors were not there; only the young couple remained.

Telepathically, I explained I was not there to harm or judge them but to help them to the threshold of Heaven. The pair gratefully and easily went with my Spirit Guide and me to the entrance of Heaven. They held hands as they disappeared through the gates.

14

THE MASTER OF THE HOUSE

THIS NEXT STORY occurred inside the same house as the ill-fated couple in the garden. Herein is another example of our personalities remaining the same when we pass as they were when we were alive.

The master bedroom was enormous and situated at the far end of one wing of the expansive manor. It was a large room on the second floor with an ornate fireplace. A door to the left of the fireplace led to a balcony with a spectacular view of Long Island Sound. In this bedroom, Joanne and Ed's two sons slept. Often, the boys would complain and blame each other for leaving the porch door open, especially in winter. What the boys did not realize at the time was that neither of them had touched the door. The boys were frequently awakened in the middle of the night by knocking on the porch door. Joanne had called me to let me know her boys were hearing strange noises in their bedroom. I tuned in to my Guide and viewed the series of events in my mind's eye via the movie they showed me.

The scene Spirit showed me was of the previous family who had hosted the party in the 1920s referred to in the story of the ill-fated couple. A very wealthy man, his wife, children, and servants lived on the estate. The man of the house slept alone in the master bedroom where the boys were now. His wife's bedroom was in the opposite wing of the house, a good distance away from his. Just outside the master bedroom is a door that leads to a staircase up to the maids' quarters on the third floor. Spirit explained that on too many nights, the husband would climb the stairs and rape one of the women servants in her small bedroom. The poor women never told anyone for fear of losing her job or even her life!

Remaining emotionally impartial can be incredibly difficult for me when I witness some of the injustices of the past. This was one of those times. Centering my thoughts and feelings through deep, controlled breaths helped me to separate myself from the events of the past and the purpose I am here to serve in the present. I had to stay calm and focused on my purpose of ridding these ghosts from my friend's house.

Seated in a chair outside on the balcony, smoking a cigar, was the man's imperious spirit. Telepathically, I began to speak to him, when he interrupted me and, in a menacing tone, said, "Who the hell do you think you are?"

Before I could answer, my Spirit Guide whisked the spirit outside and up to the highest pitch of the roof! My Guide is very protective of me and will not tolerate spirits who are rude. I was not privy to the conversation my Guide had with the "man of the house"; however, he persuaded him to go to the Other Side. My Guide explained that the arrogant spirit was always used to being the boss and getting his way. This lout had no respect for women, nor did he trust me, so my Guide felt it imperative to intervene on my behalf.

After his departure, I felt drawn to investigate the third floor. With the eclipsing personality of the master of the house removed, the spirit of the timid maid, Anna, appeared in the small bedroom. Anna wanted to tell me her heartbreaking story and release the intimate pain that had frozen her in this time and place with the abominable man. He had come to her room five nights out of seven without the wife's knowledge. She never felt safe enough to confide in anyone during her lifetime, so it was a relief to finally unload her burden on me nearly ninety years later. Anna knew I was there to help her even before I told her. Her sisters were joyfully waiting to welcome her with open arms as she crossed happily and finally into Heaven. I was so happy to see them all waving excitedly back at me before they disappeared.

A particularly difficult part of my job is to facilitate a spirit's transition without judging them, no matter their behavior. I would have liked to take Anna up before the onerous master; however, strong personalities, even in death, will overshadow other spirits and must be addressed first. While fairness dictates the victim should be taken care of before the offender, often the spirit does not feel safe until the wrongdoer is gone.

Joanne and Ed felt the energy in the master bedroom their sons shared was a lot lighter. The boys were no longer bothered by knocking in the middle of the night, and the door to the outside porch remained closed.

15

THE CRANKY OLD MAN

A MEAN-SPIRITED, CROTCHETY OLD MAN was awakening a husband and wife while they slept. They could hear him cursing and yelling at them to leave his house, and he threatened to harm them! He was also harassing and scaring the children—two daughters, aged eight and five, and a four-year-old son. The spirit threatened them all with his belligerent cursing and taunts. There was also a four-year-old spirit who played with their son, Ben. Ben could see the little boy spirit and told his parents that he loved to play with his friend. Three other spirit children were bound to the old man.

He was demanding and very possessive of the spirit children, who were petrified of this mean-old-man spirit. He hid them behind him and would not let me near them. I tried to reach the children, but he would not allow it. I knew that to contact the spirit children, I needed to confront him first.

Movie time! My Guide then showed me the man's life. It was the 1800s, and he was dressed in old rags, wearing a decrepit hat, with no teeth, and looked as though he had never bathed. His dilapidated shack on the top of a small rise was the only structure for as far as the eye could see. He kept yelling at me, "This is my property. Now get off my land!"

After a deep breath, I reached out and said I was not there to hurt him or threaten his land. I explained to him that, first of all, he was dead; second, the year was 2009; and third, I could help him. He did not believe in an afterlife or that it was 2009. He told me he was not going anywhere with me. I asked my Guide to bring a familiar spirit, a friend or anyone he liked from his time whom he might want to see and be with in Heaven. Two gentlemen showed up to talk to him, and they were dressed just like him! The three looked like something out of an old Wild West movie. He was so incredulous to see his old pals that he wept with joy. Immediately, he went with them to the Other Side without a backward glance.

After he left, the children knew I could help them see their families also in Heaven. Their parents, in spirit, came to help them cross over. I was able to bring up the three children who had been unwillingly attached to the old man. The four-year-old spirit boy did not want to leave his playmate, Ben. He loved playing with Ben and his toys because they were the same age and had become best friends. I could not persuade him to go with me. In fact, the spirit boy hid from me under the front porch outside while Ben sat in a chair on the porch with a haughty look on his face! They were colluding to stay together despite different planes of existence. Clearly, the playful personality of childhood remains as intact as a crotchety old man one does! I told the family there was nothing else I could do and took my leave, thinking that the spirits who truly needed my help had received it. I was wrong.

Later that night, I was home asleep in my bed, one hundred miles away, when my Spirit Guide awakened me at 3 a.m. Movie time, again! Spirit showed me the little four-year-old spirit sleeping in the middle of Ben's room on top of Ben's toys. Together, my Guide and I created a column of white light over the sleeping spirit and shuttled him up the warm light to his parents in Heaven.

I could not wait to call Ben's mom the next morning to tell her about the little spirit who went to Heaven in the middle of the night.

16

SEA CAPTAIN - BUSY PORT

A CLIENT CALLED TO ASK if I could help her with the many strange noises in her large house in Connecticut on Long Island Sound. The house is situated on the end of large peninsula that juts out into the water. Spirit showed me what the grounds and area looked like back in the settlers' time in the 1700s. It was the first house and a main port as you approached land by sea. It was a busy area with small farms and houses, and hundreds of ghosts were stuck around the grounds.

The first spirit my Guide showed me was inside the large house owned by a sea captain from the seventeenth century. He was the former owner of the house and most of the surrounding area. Off the kitchen, up a small flight of stairs, was the servants' room from that time. I found a teenage girl, in spirit, crouched in the corner of the room. The owner had repeatedly sexually assaulted and abused the poor girl. He was not only the master of the house but master of the surrounding farms in the area, and what he said was law. He controlled whether a person lived or died. Despite the fact that the sea captain's spirit had departed upon his death, the young girl's spirit remained stuck in the bedroom. She told me she was afraid to leave the house because she feared the master would beat her as he had done so many times. For hundreds of years, she felt unworthy to leave for fear of being judged a whore, even though the abuse was not her fault. She told me that when she died, she had ignored the white light and her family members on the Other Side who tried to coax her to go to them. I reassured her the sea captain was long gone and she had done nothing wrong. I tried to provide solace by letting her know my benevolent Guide and I had her best interests at heart. When we got to the threshold, she saw her family and friends greet her with smiling, loving faces and embraces. She ran to them.

It saddens me to meet victims with broken spirits from physical abuse. They possess zero self-esteem and no self-worth and are stuck on the Earth plane for a long time. I try not to judge the actions of degenerates like the sea captain, but as a woman, it is difficult. My Guide and I gently pleaded with her and tried to boost her morale by saying how brave and blameless she was and to let go of harsh self-judgment. It was so gratifying to help her after what she had endured for centuries.

The next spirit I encountered on this property was a married woman with her back to me, gazing out to the Sound. I learned from my Guide she was waiting for her ten-year-old daughter. While her husband was at sea, the married woman had thwarted the advances of the sea captain. As a punishment, he locked her daughter in the cellar of his house and left the child to die.

Even in death, the mother could not rescue her daughter, nor could the daughter escape; they were stuck in their emotionally charged conditions. They had both died terrified of the sea captain. Although he was no longer on the property, they were trapped by their fear of him. The mother must have died outside the building where the cellar was. The fear in their hearts and minds paralyzed them to remain in that situation until my Guide and I broke them free.

I climbed down the cellar stairs and gently approached the little girl. She was huddled next to an old chimney, trying to hide from me. I told her I was there to help reunite her with her mother. She came outside to where her mother was standing, waiting for her. They embraced for a long time, and their fear melted away. Hand-in-hand, they went together to Heaven with my Guide and me.

So often, the spirits I meet don't know they are dead. The mother of the little girl knew she was deceased but would not leave her daughter. They both had remained in spirit locked in their time for hundreds of our years. What a show of a mother's love to remain on the Earth plane to wait. How horrible and sad for the little girl to be stuck in the cellar. It was a beautiful sight to see them reunited.

A huge field of corn was the next scene I was shown, and in it were freed slaves sitting in the sun. The time period had changed, and the land looked different, but the location was the same. It was unclear how the freed slaves came to be on this land or how they died, but I knew they needed my help. My Guide would often only tell me what I needed to know. I do not like to know the specifics of the hardships many spirits had to endure in life. For instance, I knew the maid had endured abuse, but I was not privy to the minutiae. Similarly, I knew these people had been slaves, but I was not shown the particulars. From a distance, the freed slaves had watched me help the servant girl, the mother, and the child, so they were receptive when I reached out to them. I told the group of about thirty men that they were deceased and I could help them to rejoin their friends and family in the afterlife. They were ready to go and eagerly transitioned to the threshold of Heaven. It was a happy time to bring them all across.

Hurricane Sandy left the present-day owners with not only four feet of water in their basement but also a rowdy group of sailors! I was surprised how many old seafaring swashbucklers—stuck out at sea for years—had washed ashore during the hurricane! There were hundreds of them on the property. What a noisy bunch they were, but they were all too happy to go to Heaven's gate. I half expected to meet the spirit of the bellicose sea captain, but he was nowhere on the property.

It was interesting to bring so many spirits across in the same place and on the same day, yet from several different periods. Each person or group had been stuck in their individual times. Unless we choose to cross at the time of our passing, we remain suspended in time on the second, hour, and day we take our last breath.

17

———

WOMAN INSIDE A WALL

Susan and her husband, Nick, had lived in their newly-renovated home for only three months. The four-bedroom, two-hundred-year-old, colonial-style house was near the Long Island Sound in Connecticut. Susan, a sensitive lady in her mid-thirties, explained that soon after they started living there, she felt a woman's presence watching her. Her suspicions were confirmed one night when she saw the spirit of a woman wearing a long dress standing in the hallway outside her bedroom. Susan closed and locked the door because she was frightened and thought she could separate herself from the ghost. The next night, Nick woke to see a woman standing at the foot of his bed, staring at him! He was startled and yelled out. When he yelled, the ghost disappeared. He slept in another bedroom after that.

My Guide switched on a scene from the 1870s. A husband and wife were arguing upstairs in the hallway. The husband was tall and demonstrative, with an overbearing demeanor. They were both dressed in evening clothes from the Victorian period. She was overly thin and slight, wearing a long dress with beads around her neck, and her hair was high on her head in a bun. He wore a dress suit with a white shirt and an ornate high collar. It seemed they had come home from a party. Suddenly, the husband hit the wife over the head with a heavy bronze vase from a nearby table. The wife collapsed on the floor. He was glad to be rid of her and held no remorse. In the basement was a small room where he put her body and then built a wall around it.

Upon entering the house, I was immediately drawn to the upstairs hallway. Instinctively, I put my hand on an inside wall and sensed that a woman in spirit was trapped inside! Susan explained that this particular wall had been an outside wall before renovations. In the basement, I spoke to the lady spirit, told her what year it was, and that I wanted to help her. She told me her name was Virginia, and after her husband had knocked her out, she woke up inside the wall! She could not get out, and her screams fell on deaf ears. She eventually died. She wasn't afraid of me but seemed reticent and shy. I was relieved her husband wasn't lurking in the house, or I would have had to help him too. No one ever knew he murdered her and buried her in the wall. Her husband told the neighbors she had visited her close sister in Philadelphia. He sold the house and moved away soon after.

We went outside into the backyard and were assisting her to the gateway when fifty or more boisterous sailors in spirit showed up from the front of the house and surrounded us! A few weeks before, Susan had four feet of water in her basement from Hurricane Sandy. Many old sailors in spirit had been washed ashore from Long Island Sound. I explained to them that they were dead, what year it was, and that we could help them to Heaven. I said Virginia had waited a long time and would go to the head of the line to the gate of Heaven. I held Virginia's hand, and the sailors respectfully formed a line behind us. I stepped to the side to let them all pass through the entrance to Heaven. Virginia was met by her happy sister, who had been waiting for her for a long time.

My Guide said our next stop was the shoreline of Long Island Sound, less than one mile from the house. I learned that when there's a storm at sea, any souls who have died at sea can be washed ashore. There were hundreds of spirits there on the beach. My Guide and I brought them over too.

A week after I had been to Susan's house, she awoke during the night to see a woman in spirit hovering above her husband! Susan recognized the woman as his deceased grandmother; she had loved Nick very much and wanted to see him again. When Susan saw his grandmother, she shook Nick awake. They were shocked to see her and had no idea what to do. They sat up in bed, staring at her. Susan said the grandmother apologized for scaring them both, then she disappeared. The grandmother had come from Heaven to visit her grandson.

Our deceased loved ones who have been to Heaven often come back to visit us whether or not we are aware of their presence. Also, deceased family members can and do become our Guardian Angels. I know both of my deceased parents watch over me. My father gives me hints regarding my health, and my mother gives spiritual guidance—an unusual role for her since she was very Catholic, and I suspected she would not approve of me helping or believing in spirits. But happily I was wrong because now she helps me. We think we have figured out everything about someone, but that is far from the truth. I am willing to bet that loving members of your family watch over you too!

Each of us is born with at least two Guardian Angels to protect us, especially in times of trouble. For instance, when I was eight years old, I tripped on the top stair and fell headfirst down the flight of stairs. At the bottom was a cement wall. As I fell, I felt my Guardian Angel pick me up and float me gently to the bottom. I was not hurt at all. At the very least, I should have sustained a head injury or at the most, death. I did not realize what had happened to me at the time. It was not until years later, when I thought about the incident, I suspected my Guardian Angel had been there to save me from certain dangerous injury. They stay by our side from our birth to our death. Even you.

I feel a distinct difference in energy between a soul who has been to Heaven and a soul who has not. The energy feels heavier and looks denser for the ones who have not crossed over. The ones who have been there feel light and look etheric. As is my custom, I return to a client's house to be sure it is clear. When I walked into Susan's house, I sensed that Virginia was gone and no one else was in the home. Both Susan and Nick reported they were sleeping through the night without noises or seeing apparitions.

18

THE PHOTO

G OD, HELP ME!" is a common phrase uttered by many. "Someone, help me" is very different energetically. The former brings in a higher dimensional being, whereas the latter appeals to any spirit who may be close by and not necessarily benevolent. The words we use, and the intentions behind them, really matter. "Anyone, help me" opens all doors to lower vibrational entities who can leach off one's energy, as opposed to a presence who could actually help. Spirits are around us all the time. Like attracts like. If one asks for help out of desperation, shows weakness of character, and lacks self-awareness, lower energies will be attracted to that request. Be sure you ask with the highest intentions for the greatest good so you can attain spiritual guidance instead of what happened to the woman in our next story.

Ginny was depressed when she began studying medicine at nineteen years old, a profession she did not want to pursue—nor did she enjoy. Her parents insisted that all their children become doctors to achieve independence and take care of themselves financially. Ginny was now thirty-five years old and a doctor, but since moving away from her parents in Brazil to the United States, she began rebelling. Her behavior went from quiet, reserved, and shy to despondent and reckless, taking drugs and hanging out with dangerous people.

Elle was the eldest of the five girls, who all became doctors. Ginny was her baby sister and very concerned about her behavior. Ginny was not open to meeting with me in person. To help her, I asked Elle for a photograph of Ginny. I have the ability, when working with my Guide, to look at a photograph of a person and talk to their higher self. This was the stream of spirit consciousness I heard from Ginny's picture.

"Ginny was raised in a very spoiled and indulged manner. Parents pushed a high level of education on all the children to become doctors. But now she is on a destructive path and needs to hit rock bottom. She's happiest outside in nature—among the trees, grass, and natural surroundings—at a park or a beach. She needs to sit and listen so she can find her way back to her normal self. She has a chemical imbalance. She needs to calm down, and has a very excitable personality. Little things set her off, and she can not control herself. Once the agitation starts, it takes over her other feelings. She needs to love herself. She thinks no one understands who she is. She is headed for a breakdown, then afterward, she can rebuild herself back up. Meanwhile, she is frustrated. She needs to calm down. She is unhappy in her profession. She doesn't want to be a doctor any more. Had pain and hurt from childhood—high expectation was demanded of her to succeed professionally in a career and be independent in life."

It was fragmented and unclear, and I sensed someone else talking over her thoughts. I had to let the words and images come without judgment and not try to make sense of what I heard in the moment. I wrote things down as fast as I could. Soon I realized there were two spirits talking to me, and I needed to talk to them one at a time. A male personality interrupted and interjected his own opinion about Ginny. I tried to isolate the messages from him first because his personality was the stronger of the two.

My Guide explained that Ginny's uncle from Brazil was "on" Ginny. The name that came through was Vernian. Her uncle was a depressive, negative opportunist who attached himself easily to her. He latched onto her to keep himself going. He kept her down. He was the cause of her agitation and helped create more agitation. Her took over her spirit and could control her feelings.

Vernian admitted that he had attached his spirit to hers when she was nineteen, the same year he died! He was an agitated, unhappy person in life and was not going to move on anywhere. He wanted more of life and could pressure her to choose relationships with "low-life" types of people who brought her down instead of uplifting her. He manipulated her at a vulnerable time in her life, living far from home for the first time. Although Vernian had attached himself to her long ago, she could fight off his power more easily with her parents' support and influence close by. Now that they were a continent away, he had her all to himself. She became self-destructive, just as he had been in his life.

My Guide and I talked with Vernian and explained it was time for him to be on his own and move on to Heaven. Fortunately, Vernian agreed with me, and we were successful in bringing his soul to the gateway to cross into Heaven. He put up little resistance to leaving Ginny once we pointed out the negative impact he was having on his poor niece. He had a semblance of decency because he did feel guilty. Sometimes simply pointing out the "high road" is enough encouragement for spirits to be motivated to take it.

I called Elle to tell her that Ginny's spirit would be lighter, and she would think more clearly and, in time, be like her old self. Elle confirmed her uncle's name was Vernian, and he had died when Ginny was nineteen. She was surprised to learn he had been "attached" to her for fifteen years. It gave her an idea of what had been disturbing her innocent youngest sister. Today, Ginny's mind and emotions are free and unhampered by her negative uncle's spirit.

This is a prime example of the law of attraction. In the realm of our emotions, we must realize and be aware that "like attracts like." In other words, if you are a sad person, you have a greater chance of attracting sad spirits. If you are a happy person, you will attract happy spirits. If you are an angry person, you may attract angry spirits. If you are a loving person, you will attract loving spirits, and so on. The kind of energy you embody makes a huge difference.

It is imperative to our well-being to be vigilant and keenly awake to our emotions. Not only aware of our emotions but in control of them. "Think happy thoughts" is not just for Peter Pan; it is a protection from vulnerability to lower vibrational negative spirits. It would benefit all of us to consciously direct our thoughts toward a higher level of positive influence. Our lives can and do run on a smoother course when we consciously switch on a positive outlook and adopt an attitude of gratitude. In Ginny's case, when she was nineteen, she had an insecure attitude about herself, and this made her an easy target for a depressive spirit, such as her Uncle Vernian, to attach to her.

19

JAN AND THE
CRANKY BUILDER

I WAS CALLED TO JAN'S one-hundred-year-old home because her eight-year-old son, Adam, had heard voices in his bedroom over the past several months. The most recent time, he had been chased out of his bedroom by a male voice screaming at him to "get out!" As a result, he would only sleep in his parents' room.

I walked through the house, beginning with the attic. When I looked out the window, I saw the spirits of several Native Americans in the corner of the yard. As we all know, the Native Americans were on this soil long before our arrival. Many Native American ancestors have remained here in spirit on the land for centuries. Their sacred burial grounds are in our forests, cities, and backyards all over the United States. Many choose to remain on the land. As a "peace offering" and out of respect and gratitude, I brought loose tobacco for them and sprinkled it in the four corners of the property. Tobacco was a sacred plant to the Native Americans, and it was a way to acknowledge their continued presence, honor their seniority, and pay tribute.

My first encounter with Native American spirits was during a drum circle. I was shown in my mind's eye a section of the earth. The land began to lift up all in one piece, but it wasn't soil; it was many Native American spirits, interlocked like puzzle pieces, that composed the expanse. They wanted me to know that they literally make up the ground beneath our feet.

Inside the house, I noticed a difference in the atmosphere between the old part and the newer addition. The atmosphere felt heavier to me in the older section. Jan explained that her father-in-law had built an addition to the house sixty years prior.

Suddenly a man's voice spoke to me and said, "They did not need to add those rooms both upstairs and down."

I gently told him the house had new owners. As I approached the basement, the cranky old man started cussing at me and calling me nasty names. My Guide protects me from mean spirits and does not allow any spirit to be rude to me. As a result, my Guide whisked the spirit through the walls leading to the outside. I went outside and cajolingly spoke to the cranky spirit. I said I wanted to help him and could escort him to a better place where he could be with his deceased relatives and friends.

As most spirits like to tell their side of the story, this ghost wanted to share his. He wanted me to know he had built the dwelling himself and was very proud of the original house. He loved it there and did not want anyone else living inside his home, be it a relative or not. I broke the news to him that he was deceased and many years had passed since he built the house and had been alive there. I watched him absorb this information as he walked over and stood close to the six Native American warriors sitting in a circle around a campfire, smoking a pipe. I asked the old man if he wanted me to bring him over first. He answered that the Native American's were his friends. He felt it was his function to look after them, and he felt protective of them! He wanted the Native Americans to go first before my Guide and I brought him over. I politely addressed the warriors and asked if they would like to move on to a higher realm. My Guide translates my intentions so they may understand. I was not privy to the conversation between my Guide and the spirit warriors, but I saw the results in the reactions of the spirits. My Guide formed a cylinder of white light in the center of the yard that reached to the sky and yet was connected to the ground. It looked like a vertical tractor beam, similar to the one from *Star Trek*. The warriors stood and followed each other into the column of light to the gateway. The old man seemed happier and calmer after seeing his friends go into the cylinder of light. Finally, it was his turn to go. I asked the Spirit World to please bring his family and friends from inside Heaven. I could see a group of smiling people waiting for him as he passed over to them.

Young Adam went back to sleeping in his own bedroom since there was no one else to bother him.

The thing is that Earth is not our origin of home. Heaven is our true home, and we all have the ability and right to return there when we die.

20

———

PLAYFUL LITTLE GHOST GIRL

J AN (FROM THE PREVIOUS STORY) lived in a house briefly in a small suburb of New York City in the 1970s. She relayed an experience she had there when she was little, aged five. Jan and her older sister shared a bedroom in the attic. At night when she got into bed, a little ghost girl her age would appear. Jan could see and hear her, but her older sister could not. She would freeze with the covers tucked under her chin, too scared to say anything or tell anyone what she saw and heard. At night, the little ghost girl would fly around her room and say, "I'm over here." Then she would fly to another spot in the attic and say, "Now I'm over here." Jan never spoke to the ghost, and she and her family moved away a few years later.

Jan always wondered if the ghost girl had moved with her to their new home, even though she could no longer see or hear her. She asked if I would go to her old house to find out if the little ghost girl was still there.

I tuned into my Guide, who said the little girl was still on the property, even though they had torn down Jan's old house and built a new one in its place. I drove up to the old address and parked a little way down the road. I saw the little ghost girl high in a tree in the front yard of the new house. She was playing and appeared happy and in good spirits (no pun intended). I spoke to her and told her about Jan, who was grown up now and had sent me here to help her. She was happy and unsurprised to see me; in fact, she seemed to be expecting me. My Guide said the Spirit World makes the arrangements; I merely have to show up.

My Guide explained that in the 1950s, her mother poisoned her, and she died in the original house on the property. The little girl never knew her mother had murdered her; she was only five years old when she died. This was the only place she knew, and she had nowhere else to go. She had never left the property from when she died until we took her to Heaven some sixty years later. I asked the Spirit World to bring someone who loved her to be there for her. She recognized her grandmother waiting for her. Happily, she waved good bye to me and skipped into her grandmother's open arms.

21

———

PARKING LOT TRAGEDY

ETTY OWNS A BEAUTY SALON in a small town in Connecticut. Her shop is located on a busy street with bars and restaurants and a lively nightlife. Most weekend nights, the bars are open until 2:00 a.m. One such night, two young women were partying in one of the bars until closing. Their car was parked in a small municipal parking lot behind Betty's beauty shop. At night, the lot is not well-lit, and the street lights are spaced far apart. The parking spaces are crammed together, and the area between the three rows of parked cars is narrow and at an angle. All of these things led to the tragedy that was about to unfold. Both girls were drunk, and one of them had just turned twenty-one. One of the girls sat in the area between the two rows of cars. According to her friend, she was having a "temper tantrum" and would not get up. A gentleman from one of the nearby restaurants had just finished work and was anxious to get home after his long shift. The newspapers said he never saw her sitting in the dark parking lot when he drove over her and dragged her for twenty feet. The other girl ran after his car, screaming at him to stop. Tragically, her friend died on the way to the hospital.

Betty asked me to check the parking lot behind her beauty salon to see if the poor girl's spirit was still there. My Guide said she was and needed my help. I parked in the lot and walked around to see where she was. When I found her, she was sitting on the ground, dazed and confused, and did not know what had happened to her or where she was. She had not felt the pain or fear that her body had endured because our spirits are protected from earthly trauma at the time of death. I explained that she had passed and described the events that led to her passing. I acquainted her with the idea that she was between worlds and asked if she would like my Guide and me to escort her to the gates of Heaven. She agreed, and we brought her over that day from the parking lot.

22

GRAVEYARD CHECK-INS

Anytime I drive by a graveyard, I check to see if there are spirits wanting help to the gates of Heaven. Spirits do not necessarily hang out in graveyards, but the location has become a "way station" my Guide uses for me to find them. I have developed a habit of tuning in as I encounter cemeteries, and my Guide has become accustomed to this pattern of behavior. You can liken it to leaving a basket of folded laundry on the stairs: you know the next person who goes up will inevitably encounter said basket and hopefully bring it up. In the same way, when I pass a graveyard, I am reminded to check in.

I was staying overnight with relatives in a suburb five miles outside of Boston. It was a beautiful spring day, perfect for a walk. A walking path a few miles long circled the lake, and several burial grounds from different religions dotted the shores. Being alone, I tuned into my Guide to ask if any deceased souls needed to cross over. As it turns out, together, we crossed hundreds of deceased spirits from different eras that day. It was a very busy place for spirits—both religious and non-believers. The most surprising thing was witnessing many spirits rise from the lake and come toward me! I was unaccustomed to seeing apparitions pop out of a body of water. This job always springs eternal newness.

As I walked toward the first graveyard, I noticed it was very old, with barely readable markers from the Puritan days of the late 1600s. As I began a mental conversation asking if any spirits would like to accompany my Guide and me, the Puritans' personalities grew indignant and stern. They mumbled together that I was a witch! The Puritans made it clear they did not trust me and were not about to go with me. I felt there was more behind their scorn, and when I gently probed, the spirits admitted they were fearful and felt unworthy to go to Heaven. Having lived their lives in an extremely harsh religion that demanded perfection with no tolerance for mistakes, their spirits chose to stay where they were rather than face the devil or hell they had been promised. Some of them came with us, but some remained and, to my knowledge, are there still.

I stopped for a break after the oppressive energy of the Puritan cemetery. I closed my eyes, took deep breaths, and did a quick clearing meditation to reground myself. As I opened my eyes and gazed over the sparkling water, a large group of spirits floated up out of the lake and came toward me! They had witnessed my exchange with the Puritans and knew my intentions. The spirits arrived at my side, ready to cross through Heaven's gateway.

In the same vicinity was a Jewish cemetery. Many small stones adorned the tops of the headstones. Spirits were sitting on top of their graves or standing in groups talking. The energy here was quite different from the burial ground of the Puritans. It was much more relaxed and jovial. I reached out to them and asked if anyone would like to go on to the gateway to Heaven. They were delighted and joined the numbers in crossing over.

When I started the walk around this busy town lake, I had no expectations that so many deceased souls would be in the area. It is amazing and gratifying to help so many souls at once. No matter what religion you follow on Earth, we are all one in our humanity— all can return to our origin of source if we believe we can and that we are worthy.

23

ELSA

MY MOTHER AND I went to church for Sunday mass when we visited one another in Florida. A neighbor and close friend of my mother's, Elsa, had died a few months earlier. We went to the same church Elsa had frequented for many years. Suddenly, while kneeling in the pew, I saw Elsa's spirit flying around the ceiling, high above the altar. My mother did not know of my ability to see spirits as her Catholic faith would have prevented her from accepting it. Unfortunately, this was a conversation we had never had in life. I knew I had to help our old neighborhood friend. I closed my eyes and began talking to Elsa, who was astounded I could see and talk to her. She was very upset and confused and didn't know where she was, but she felt safe in the familiar surroundings of the church she had frequented.

Elsa had gone to mass every Sunday and every day prayed the Rosary, but when it came time to go into the light once she passed, she said she could not do it. She didn't tell me her reasons, but I have a hunch that, like many of us brought up in the Catholic faith (no offense), she felt unworthy of going to Heaven

Meanwhile, my mother kept nudging me to stand up or kneel down as the mass dictated. She did not want me to close my eyes because she thought I was not paying attention. It was pretty comical. After Elsa and I conversed for a bit longer, despite my mother's earthly interruptions, she told me she did indeed want to go to Heaven to be with her adoring husband, Tony. My Guide and I watched as Tony waited for her, and they were both relieved that she had finally made it.

My greatest hope for writing these stories is to convey to you that not only does life go on, but also we have every right to be happy and with our loved ones in Heaven after we pass. Living a life on Earth is wonderful in so many ways, but none of us escapes trials and hardships. I believe we are here to love and help one another. We all help and love one another in some way, but as we review the acts of our lives after death, we may feel we fall short of what we had been told was expected of us. My life's work is to help spirits mired in this feeling of inadequacy to realize the mere fact of being here on Earth constitutes worthiness to graduate after their bodily death.

24

MUSCLE CAR SHOW

ON A SUNNY AFTERNOON in Florida, along a main drag, my husband and I stopped at a car show—there were the cool fast cars of the 1960s. Being from the generation when muscle cars were the rage, it was fun to walk around to view them. Most of the cars had the windows down to allow people to peek in to view the spick-and-span interiors. When I poked my head into a small black corvette, I immediately felt an overwhelming, negative thick dark energy swimming around my head. My head felt engulfed in an invisible miasma, and I was instantly nauseous.

A nasty spirit yelled, "Get out of my car!" Surprised, I jerked my head back out of the car. The fresh air helped me feel better, but it took several minutes for my head to clear.

I tuned in to my Spirit Guide to get the scoop on this coupe. My Guide informed me this ghost had died in his car while he was drag racing with friends in the early 1960s. He was angry that he had died and furious that someone else had the nerve to buy his car. The new owner had restored it, which incensed him all the more. This was an example of a spirit who chose at his death to stay with an object—in this case, his favorite car.

My Guide protected my head with an abundance of small white feathery wings to dispel the negativity. I could feel and see them in my mind's eye. I gathered up white light into a ball and hurled it into the car, watching the dark energy shrink and move into the back seat. As I approached the car, but did not put my head inside, I could see the darkness diminish, but it did not disappear.

I told the ghost, as he shriveled in the back of the car, that I could help him go to Heaven's entrance.

He said, "This is my car, and I am not going anywhere with you!"

As far as I know, that angry former owner is still with his car. He made it clear to my Guide and me that he was not ready to go into the light nor move anywhere else.

As I have mentioned, no one can force anyone to move on until their spirit is ready. Anger is a powerful emotion and can be all-consuming, as with this spirit. I do not engage angry spirits who are unwilling to change. The only way to combat anger is to have no fear and send love and light, then walk away and leave it alone. I walked away and left him alone.

25

THE LITTLE PLAYMATE

T IS NOT UNUSUAL FOR CHILDREN to see, notice, and play with children in spirit. The above story, "The Cranky Old Man," had the four-year-old spirit who played with gentle Ben and his toys. This next story illustrates a distant cousin who never left the property and befriended my friend's son for many years.

Lisa asked me to come to her house; she suspected she had a ghost. She told me she would see things out of the corner of her eye and hear odd noises when no one else was home. She said the center of this spirit activity came from her son's bedroom. When I walked into Jon's bedroom, a young man of fifteen years in spirit flew through the closed window into the shed in their backyard. I went to the window and tried to communicate with him, but he did not respond and wanted no part of me.

My Guide informed me the ghost's name was Peter, a distant cousin who died young two hundred years earlier. The property had been in Lisa's husband's family since the early 1800s. She, her husband, and their two children were the current descendant residents.

I asked Jon, a high school student, if he ever sensed anyone in his bedroom. Jon was surprised I asked and confessed to his mother and me that when he was a young boy, he had a companion with whom he would talk in the middle of the night. They would play games together and have long conversations.

Lisa was shocked that her son had never mentioned it before now. She said, "I had no idea this had been happening for years."

Jon said he thought no one would believe him about growing up with an "invisible friend." Many children keep quiet about seeing spirits for fear of being ridiculed and not believed. I hope that changes one day.

Years went by until, one day, Lisa asked me to return to her house. She was seeing things, and her daughter, Alice, was upset her toiletries were being moved around in her bathroom. As I sat in their kitchen, I could see a young man in spirit leaning in the doorway. He indicated he wanted me to accompany him, so I followed him upstairs to Jon's bedroom. This time when I entered Jon's bedroom, I loudly heard the spirit lament, "He's not coming back this time! He won't be coming back!" He thought he was losing Jon forever. Peter had watched Jon grow up from an infant in to a man.

Jon had graduated from law school and recently moved out of his family's house to an apartment with his fiancé. Over the years, he had moved out temporarily but always came home. Peter eagerly welcomed him back, but this time, he knew his best friend and cousin would not return. Peter was upset at the thought of not seeing him again. I explained that he could come back anytime he wished to visit Jon once he crossed into Heaven.

Peter told his story: When he was sixteen, he had accidentally fallen from a hayloft in a barn on the property. He remained on the property for two hundred years. When Jon was born, he was ecstatic to have a playmate. Peter loved Jon deeply and identified with him as the man he might have been—had he lived. They were very close, but Peter knew it was time for him to move on when he realized Jon would not move home again.

He understood I could help him since I wanted to years earlier, so he made himself known to Lisa and Alice by moving objects and being seen out of the corner of Lisa's eye. This is a very common way spirits make themselves known. When you see something out of the corner of your eye, appearing like a shadowy figure, it is most likely a ghost or spirit.

I explained to Peter that he could come back anytime to see Jon's progress. Knowing this made him happy, and my Guide and I escorted him to Heaven that day, along with other relatives who showed up to help him cross.

When I called Jon, he was sad about losing his childhood friend, who was like the brother he never physically had. However, there was good news—my Spirit Guide told me Peter would be assigned as Jon's additional Guardian Angel for the rest of his life. They were ecstatic at that news. I explained how they could talk through writing and mental telepathy.

"All's well that ends well."
—*William Shakespeare, my hero.*

26

THE FRENCH ATHLETE

W HEN OUR TIME IS UP, IT IS UP. I believe the end of our life is predetermined by our soul, and the soul decides when it is over. Each lifetime comes with instructions for the mission we must fulfill for our soul's growth. Unfortunately, our conscious mind does not remember making that pact nor what that mission is! The pact was made before we arrived on Earth. Your mission could be as simple as smiling at the right person at the right time on the right day. It is not as complicated as we humans might think. It is not about notoriety or grandiose gestures. It comes down to how we love ourselves and treat each other and our relationships as we work on our forgotten missions synchronistically.

Most of the spirits I encounter are upset that suddenly their lives are over. Their consciousness does not recall the pact they made because their spirit has not returned home to reconnect and remember.

Early one morning, a healthy, fit woman in her early fifties went for a run, came home, then snorkeled in the Caribbean sea right outside her bungalow. My Guide said she had a heart attack while snorkeling and was dead by 10:30 a.m. My husband and I walked by the bungalow as the police spoke with her husband. The ambulance had already taken her body away. Her husband sat on a bench outside their bungalow with his head in his hands, crying. I looked over and heard her panicked, confused voice speaking to him in French. I did not know what she was saying, but he could not hear her. I tried to calm her down by softly explaining I could hear and see her. I relayed what had happened that morning. I don't speak French; my Guide does the translating.

She told me it was shocking for her to be in another state, as it is for most people when they die suddenly. She was desperately trying to talk to her husband but to no avail. She was frustrated and upset that she was dead, especially since she kept herself physically in shape by exercising daily. She told me she thought she had many years left.

I suggested she visit with her husband, friends, and relatives to say her goodbyes, then meet on the beach in three days, and her deceased family members would be there for her. Three days later, a special aunt whom she was close to, along with her mother, father, and other family members in spirit, helped their beloved girl. She went to Heaven and was gratefully reunited with them all.

27

———

THE GUARDIAN OF THE NATIVE AMERICANS

MELANIE SAID SHE AND HER FAMILY were being hassled by a mean spirit in their home. She lived with her teenage daughter, Alice, and her husband, Steve. She and her daughter repeatedly saw a black shadow fly through the house. Sometimes it would stop on the staircase to the second floor and "peer meanly" at them. They both thought the ghost was menacing. The spirit repeatedly went into Alice's bedroom and woke her in the middle of the night by sitting on her chest. She was scared out of her wits and could not breathe. She screamed for her mother, who would come running. The ghost would stand in the corner and glare at them both. They did not want to move since they had only been in the house a few months.

When I walked into their living room, I watched a shadow come out of the front wall and move quickly in a straight line outside to the backyard. I followed to see where he went and looked out the window to see a group of Native Americans sitting around a camp-fire. They did not acknowledge his presence as he stood guard over them, protecting them from me.

My Guide said this was a man who had been on the property for over one hundred years. As I walked through the house, Melanie asked if I knew the ghost's name.

He heard her and answered rudely, "I am Poca-f*ing-hontas."

My Guide answered, "His name was Sam."

I could feel Sam's cantankerous nature and the challenge he posed. I explained that I was there to help, not hurt him. I told him he was dead, which he seemed to already know. Sam admonished that this was his land when he was alive, one hundred and fifty years ago; before that, the land belonged to them (meaning the Native Americans). He was adamant that he was not leaving until I helped the Native Americans first. These were his friends, and he was safe-guarding them.

With the help of Spirit, we created a clear vertical cylinder filled with light in the backyard for the gentlemen around the fire. There were many Native Americans who walked into that beam; some came from the surrounding lands. After they had all gone, I told Sam it was his turn. I asked Spirit to please bring his family and friends from the Spirit World. When he saw them, he gladly went with them.

Customarily, I revisit a client's house a week later to make sure it is clear. As I got out of the car in the driveway, a group of fifty or more people in spirit started clapping to thank me for bringing Sam's stuck soul to Heaven's gate. That had never happened to me before! I felt embarrassed and shy, as I do in big groups, yet grateful I could help him and the Native Americans.

28

THE HAUNTED RESTAURANT

A DEAR FRIEND OF MINE owns a wonderful restaurant in upstate New York. She called me one day, distressed, to tell me her restaurant basement was haunted. Several times "someone" had tried to push her while she was on the old narrow staircase to the basement. Other staff members had heard "someone" yell at them to "get out!" Food stuffs flew off the shelves and nearly hit the staff. These things had been happening for months.

When I arrived, my Spirit Guide said her basement was loaded with spirits. The first person I encountered was a young man in his twenties. He had the presence of being the boss. The basement had low ceilings, with many small dark rooms connected by mini corridors. The floor was made of dirt and rock (common for a two-hundred-year-old building). At one point in the history of the building, it was used by the Underground Railroad.

I found many African-Americans in spirit huddled together in a sealed room. I was relieved to find the young male was protecting them. He was trying to shelter them from me. I explained that I wanted to help them all. I informed him that he was dead, and so were the African-Americans. They had been dead for over one hundred and fifty years, and the year was now 2016. Spirits are consistently amazed when they learn the current year. After convincing them I could bring them to their loved ones in spirit, my Guide brought their deceased relatives and friends to meet them, along with their Guardian Angels.

In another section of the basement, Native Americans sat in a circle on the dirt floor, not paying attention to me. As in previous stories, they were smoking a pipe and busy conversing amongst themselves. I sensed they knew I was there, so I began speaking to them, letting them know they were dead and what the year was. Spirit translated that I was there to help them join their ancestors. Together, once again, we created a large vertical cylinder of light that enveloped them where they were sitting. They each stood up and entered the beam of light and the next realm. In that spiritual dimension, I left the lighted cylinder in case there were other Native Americans in the area who wanted to join their ancestors.

Nearby was an open hearth made of bricks used for cooking two hundred years ago. Behind it was a very dark room with a dirt floor, a stone wall, and a small narrow opening. When I used my flashlight, I saw an old woman in spirit crouching and trying to hide by pressing her back against the far wall. Gently, I spoke to her and explained I was there to help. She told me she was born half-white and half-Native American. She had been beaten all her life by the Native Americans as she had "mixed blood." Neither side accepted her as Native American or white. She lived alone all her life but developed many talents with healing and knowledge of medicinal herbs. She told me she was very proud of herself. Together, my Guide and I happily escorted her. All her ancestors embraced her at long last. It is immensely rewarding to help someone who has suffered so much in this life to go to Heaven, whatever it may look like for them on the Other Side.

29

A SOUTH AFRICAN FAMILY PORTRAIT

This story is a cautionary tale, not set in folklore, but it does involve dangerous people. It is a preposterous-sounding story, but I assure you it happened and was very real.

Sarah was a business woman who worked for a large company in Westchester County. She lived alone in a two-story condo in a quiet neighborhood. She told me her aunt in South Africa was sending her a full-length portrait of her great-grandfather, who died in 1930. The portrait had been painted and framed in 1920. Sarah had recently inherited the portrait, but when her aunt sent her a photo of it, Sarah told me, "It gave her an uneasy feeling."

The portrait hung for years in her elderly cousin Frederick's library in his home. He was wealthy and owned a plantation in South Africa. Sarah told me the portrait had been hanging on the wall facing her cousin when he was murdered in a chair. The portrait had witnessed her cousin Frederick's murder!

Sarah relayed her story: A few weeks before his murder, Frederick had gone to his bank to withdraw $10,000 for a new wheelchair for his disabled wife. Someone working at the bank tipped off gang members about the money. The gang went to the housekeeper's home and threatened her family's lives if she did not let them into her employer's home. Frederick and his wife were both in their late eighties. When the gang came to his front door, the housekeeper let them in. They robbed the safe, raped the housekeeper, then tied Frederick up in his library where the portrait hung. Tragically, Frederick suffocated when the gang members tied his suspenders around his neck.

Initially, I asked Sarah to email a photo of the portrait. I could sense negative energy right away. I discovered two gentlemen in spirit, unrelated to her great-grandfather, also stuck in the portrait. These two had had business dealings with Sarah's great-grandfather back in the 1920s. They were unconnected to the robbery and Frederick's murder. My Guide and I were successful in assisting those two gentlemen to Heaven's gate.

A few weeks later, the portrait arrived at Sarah's condo. She said strange things began to happen immediately after she hung the portrait on the wall in the first-floor hallway. One night, as she was carrying a dinner plate full of food into her den, the plate was knocked out of her hands and onto the floor. Her dinner was ruined. That happened twice more. In another instance, she felt someone hit her on the back of her head as she got dressed upstairs. She asked me to come as soon as I could to clear the portrait. She was unable to sleep from the constant noise—strange sounds and banging all night long. She felt afraid of the malicious entity that had invaded her home—coincidentally after the portrait arrived.

The night before I went to her condo, I suggested she cover the entire portrait with a sheet. As she covered it, she heard it scream at her in one long, loud wail! As she told me this, my stomach felt queasy. Sometimes when a negative soul is involved, like this one, I will feel nauseous. I have no fear of these souls since I know I am fully protected and meant to assist them if they allow. However, Sarah's stories were unnerving, and I was less than enthusiastic about seeing her family's artwork.

The next day, I confirmed with my Spirit Guide that I was indeed intended to go and help Sarah. I sat in my car outside her condo, not knowing what to expect when I went inside. But I knew that if my Spirit Guide wanted me there, then the Spirit world had my back.

I gently took the sheet off of the portrait. Immediately, a young African man in his late teens started yelling at me. He told me he had become a new member of a notorious, malicious gang in South Africa. The gang had killed him, along with Sarah's cousin, in the same room where the portrait had hung. He had not wanted to be a part of the cousin's murder. He was "too soft," and they decided they could not trust him not to snitch on them, so they killed him. The portrait had acquired five spirits in all: the great-grandfather, Frederick, the young African man, and the two businessmen.

The African was furious and screamed at me that he hated being in New York; it was cold with too many people, and he wanted to be back in Africa! He blamed Sarah for dragging him to New York, and he insisted I send him back. I calmed him down by quietly whispering to him that he was dead and that my Guide and I could take him to the entrance to Heaven. He calmed down and agreed, especially when he realized we were trying to help him. When he saw his deceased relatives encouraging him, he acquiesced to go to them. His personality had dominated the other two spirits, so we had to transition him first.

The entire time Frederick had been attached to the portrait, the young African had bullied him. Frederick seemed a submissive spirit and was thoroughly confused. He told us his grandfather's spirit had called him into the portrait after the murder. Unfortunately, the spirit of the young African gang member, fixed itself onto the portrait at the same time. Once the young African was on the Other Side, my Guide and I could focus on Frederick and his grandfather. They were grateful to leave the portrait, and together they went to Heaven.

All five spirits had travelled with the portrait to New York and Sarah's condo. My Guide said the portrait was used as a portal for spirits, and we needed to close the portal. We did! This is an example of a spirit or spirits attaching to an object—in this case, a portrait. Photographs and portraits of people can be conduits of the soul energy of the person whose image they contain. Photos can enable contact with the spirit, regardless of whether the person is alive or passed.

To this day, the murders have not been solved. However, Sarah sleeps soundly and is not disturbed by the portrait, which still hangs in her front hall.

30

KAY

This last story shows that life continues after what we call "death."

My friend Nancy called one day to inform me her younger sister, Kay had stage four brain and breast cancer. She said Kay, at 50 years young, was in the hospital dying and would I please visit her since she could not visit her from Colorado. She asked me to help her little sister transition when she was ready to pass on to the next life.

When I saw Kay, she was in and out of consciousness because of the pain medications. Even though I had been out of touch with Kay for many years, it was as though I had seen her yesterday. With some people, the connection is so strong that you pick up right where you left off. We joked around and bantered light heartedly with three other family members who were there in support. The family was in denial that Kay was near the end of her life since she had only been diagnosed with cancer three weeks prior. The cancer was so far advanced that they were still in shock at the prospect of losing her.

I visited Kay nearly every day for two weeks. In the hospital, one afternoon, her deceased father spoke to me. He wanted to share a sweet story that happened between the two of them. He told me that when she was a little girl, he would go into her room to kiss her good-night. On one particular night, it was snowing hard outside her window, and together they made snowballs and placed them on the windowsill. They laughed as they lined snowballs up on the sill. He wanted me to remind his daughter of that precious time they shared. He said that he would be there for her when she passed on to Heaven, and I did not need to help her. Their father knew Nancy had requested my help in crossing her over, but he needed my help conveying comforting memories so he could be there for her at her moment of transition.

Kay did not know that I could help souls to Heaven. Given her Catholic faith, I think it would have freaked her out knowing I could do such a thing. I ran the risk she would not believe that I could talk with her deceased father. Instead, I told Kay I had dreamt about her father and the two making snowballs on the windowsill.

"I had the same dream!" she exclaimed. She was so excited to be reminded of that private memory on that winter night and confirmed that she felt her father around her. It confirmed to me their strong love connection in life had not diminished in death, and they would soon be reunited.

It was the last week of her hospital stay; I was standing outside Kay's room. Inside her room, the well-meaning sister-in-law was crying and arguing with the nurse over Kay's treatment. She wanted the nurse to do more for Kay, who was in great pain and calling out. Suddenly, Kay's spirit came out to the hallway to talk with me. She told me she was not in any pain; it was her body reacting to her spirit trying to let go. The scene in the room looked scary to the living, but to Kay it was akin to the transition of a woman giving birth. Transitions can look painful, but they are everywhere around us in nature. Caterpillars in a chrysalis literally liquify their bodies to become a butterfly. Kay's body was preparing for her spirit to be released.

Kay's spirit said, "My body is so tired of the pain, and my soul is ready to go."

I told her, "It is okay for you to let go. Your father will be waiting for you to cross over into Heaven."

As with many dying hospital patients, Kay needed someone to give her permission to die. She needed to hear that it was alright to leave her distraught family members. They were consumed by grief and afraid of life without her. They were unaware their energy was keeping her trapped in a dying body. On some level, they knew they could not save her, but in desperation, they were pleading with doctors and nurses to prolong her life. When this stage happens, it is best for the living to accept death to help their loved ones feel at peace with their transition.

Early the next morning, Kay was gone.

It is one of the hardest things in life to watch our loved one's body suffer and die. But accepting the body's metamorphosis and the spirit's evolution helps us to be present in the moment and hold space for our dying loved ones.

I was twenty-two when I held space for my father to take his last breath. He was fifty-four years young with lung cancer. I held his head in my hands as he passed in his bed at home. He said as he exhaled his last breath, "It's alright, Mommy." In life, Pop had been very close to his mother. I wondered for years if she had come for him on his dying day. I found out years after he died that his mother had indeed come to bring him home to Heaven. I believe most of us who have faith in Heaven—our true home—know we will return there after the thing called bodily death.

"We are not human beings having a spiritual experience.
We are spiritual beings having an earthly experience."
—*Pierre Teilhard de Chardin*

ABOUT THE AUTHOR

ANN CARROLL MARTIN was born an empath, which is the ability to sense other people's emotions. In addition, she was born with the "gift of discernment," to understand or know something through the power of the Holy Spirit. She is a Reiki Master and studied and obtained Level 3 as a Healing Touch Volunteer, sponsored by Yale New Haven Hospital. For over twenty years, she has assisted thousands of lost and confused deceased souls to a more advanced realm. She lives with her husband in the Catskill mountains in upstate New York.